Booze
Cakes

Booze Cakes

CONFECTIONS SPIKED *with* **SPIRITS**, **WINE**, *and* **BEER**

Krystina Castella *and* Terry Lee Stone

Copyright © 2010 **Krystina Castella** and **Terry Lee Stone**

Library of Congress Cataloging in Publication Number: 2009944100

ISBN: 978-1-59474-423-5

Printed in China

Typeset in Century Expanded, ITC Century, and ITC Franklin Gothic

Designed by **Jenny Kraemer**
Production management by **John J. McGurk**

Photography by **Daniel Kukla** except the following: pages 60, 70, 82,
84, 87, and 114 by Jenny Kraemer
Baking and recipe testing by **Jennifer Perillo**
www.injennieskitchen.com

Some recipes and text on pages 27, 63, 67, 76, and 96 first appeared in
Field Guide to Cocktails by **Rob Chirico**; some recipes on pages 136 to 138,
and 141 first appeared in *Field Guide to Candy* by **Anita Chu**; and some recipes
on pages 138 to 140 first appeared in *Field Guide to Cookies* by Anita Chu.
Reprinted by permission of the publisher.

Distributed in North America by Chronicle Books
680 Second Street
San Francisco, CA 94107

10 9 8 7 6 5 4 3 2 1

Quirk Books
215 Church Street
Philadelphia, PA 19106
www.quirkbooks.com
www.irreference.com

Note: All sugar is granulated, unless otherwise specified. All eggs are large. All
ingredients—including eggs, butter, and cream cheese—should be used at room
temperature for optimal results. ***Please bake responsibly!***

Contents

Introduction

Think of *Booze Cakes* as your guidebook to a brand-new baking adventure. Let us be your cruise directors and libation engineers. We are relaxed bakers—we bake for fun! We're here to counter the idea that baking is hard. In our opinion, baking is easy when you use fresh and simple ingredients, throw in some booze, pop it into the oven, and wait for the magic to happen (while enjoying a cocktail or two). These delicious tipsy confections are meant to be savored and shared.

Introduction: Booze Cakes Basics

Why Put Booze in Cake?

Cake has been around since ancient times. So has alcohol. Both are essential to nourishment, ritual, and celebration. Greeks and Romans added beer to cake as a preservative. And because beer is made from yeast, it functions as a leavening agent as well as imparting a rich flavor to baked goods.

Later, Europeans used various alcohols, such as whiskey and brandy, to spice and preserve their confections; in the 1700s, the British combined sherry, cake, and custard and the result is the tasty trifles we all know and love. Rum-infused desserts became all the rage when sugarcane made that alcohol cheap and widely available throughout the Caribbean and the Americas. In colonial America, baked cakes were drizzled with brandy liqueur and stored in a tight container until all the alcohol was absorbed, then they were drizzled with liquor and stored a few more times to produce a delicious treat that—if undecorated and wrapped airtight—could keep for *years*.

During America's Prohibition era, discretely boozy alcohol-infused cakes were popular treats among tipplers, as was the cocktail: Both used fruit and sweeteners to soften the taste of rot-gut hooch. The 1970s saw another booze-cake revival, spurred by society's permissive attitude toward mood-altering substances. Today, cocktail-cake parties are an easy way to sweeten everyday life. When the going gets rough, the tough make booze cakes!

🍶 + 🍰 = ☺

Baking with Spirits, Wine, and Beer

Baking is magic. Baking with booze is even more magic. Technically, baking is chemistry, but we don't need to get into the comprehensive scientific explanation of how baking works. There's one basic rule: Never bake with anything you wouldn't drink. Do you have to purchase premium brands? No. Just use your favorites—you'll have plenty left over for cocktails. Here's a brief overview of great baking alcohols and how they can be used to flavor cakes.

Beer

Beer is brewed from water, malted barley that's often combined with other grains, like corn, rye, or wheat, flavored with hops, a conelike flower, and fermented with yeast. Beers come in a wide range, from light to dark and from bitter to mellow. Choosing one is a matter of personal taste. Ale is a stronger version of beer, in terms of both taste and alcohol content.

Brandy

Brandy is liquor distilled from wine or fermented fruit juice that is then often aged, typically in wood, which adds color and smooths out the flavor. The word *brandy* comes from the Dutch *brandewijn*, meaning "burned (distilled) wine." Known for their aromatic qualities and rich fruity flavors, brandies can be made from almost any fruit. Some key varieties are:

Apples	Calvados, applejack
Apricots, cherries, blackberries	Apricot, cherry, and blackberry brandy
Grapes (wine)	Cognac, armagnac, grappa

Liqueurs

Liqueurs are sweetened spirits flavored with different fruits, nuts, seeds, spices, herbs, and flowers. A range of liquors are used as the spirit's base, including rum, brandy, and whiskey. Liqueurs are flavored by distillation, infusion, percolation, or maceration, each a different way of extracting the ingredients' essence and combining them with alcohol. They range from 30-proof (15 percent) to 110-proof (55 percent). Base liquors are often added to liqueurs, and cream is added to make cream liqueurs. There are generic liqueurs like anisette and proprietary, or name-brand liqueurs, such as Sambuca; some have cream added as well. The recipes in this book call for generic brands. The ones to know are:

Almonds	Amaretto
Anise	Anisette, Sambuca, Ouzo, Pastis
Banana	Crème de Banane
Cherries	Kirsch, *Kirschwasser*
Coffee	Tia Maria
Coffee & cocoa beans	Kahlúa
Hazelnut	Frangelico
Lemons	Limoncello
Mint	Crème de Menthe (clear or green)

Oranges	Cointreau, Curacao, Triple Sec, Grand Marinier
Peach liqueur & bourbon	Southern Comfort
Pomegranate	Grenadine, Pama
Raspberry	Chambord, Framboise
Various fruits and herbs	Schnapps, Galliano

Unlike sweet liqueurs, **liquors** are alcohols made of fermented grains and/or plants, such as **rum**, **brandy**, and **whiskey**. Some modern liquors are flavored, but in general liquors are not sweet.

Rum

Rum is distilled sugarcane or molasses. Originally from the West Indies but now made throughout the Caribbean, rum has a thick, sweet, mellow taste that has made it a perennial favorite for baking. It comes in several versions; which one you choose depends on how rummy-tasting you like your cakes. We specify the type of rum in our recipes, but feel free to try others:

Light	*White or silver*, clear and dry tasting
Medium	*Gold or amber*, caramel added, richer taste
Dark	*Aged or añejo*, fuller body, flavor and aroma
Spiced	Aromatic spices and flavorings added
Flavored	Light rum infused with coconut or a variety of fruits, like lemon, peach, orange

Tequila

Tequila is distilled blue agave and is made only in certain locations in Mexico, primarily surrounding the city of Tequila. By Mexican law, it must contain at least 51 percent agave; the balance typically is sugarcane. There are five categories of tequila, also regulated by law:

Blanco	*White, silver, or plata*, herbaceous and peppery
Jovenabocado	*Gold*, caramel added, richer taste
Reposado	*Rested*, usually in oak up to a year, mellow character

| Añejo | *Aged*, 1 to 3 years, smooth, complex taste |
| Extraañejo | *Extra-aged*, minimum 3 years in oak, elegant, rich |

Vodka

Vodka may be the purest, most neutral liquor; it lacks color and a distinctive aroma or taste. Although its origin is disputed—with Russia, Poland, and Scandinavia all vying for the honors—the name *vodka* comes from the Russian водка, which means "little water." Today's vodkas are a highly refined distilled combination of water and fermented grains (typically rye or wheat), potatoes, or sugar beet molasses. Flavored vodkas are available, or you can make your own (page 131).

Whiskey

Whiskey is made from a fermented mash of cereal grains (such as corn, rye, barley, oats, and wheat), along with water, malt, sugar, and yeast. The word is derived from the Gaelic *uisqebaugh* (pronounced *whiskee-RAW*), which translates as "water of life." Ingredients, distillation method, and aging techniques all change a whiskey's flavor, ranging from sweet to earthy to smoky. Some whiskeys are blended; those that aren't are known as straight whiskey. In small amounts, one whiskey can be substituted for another; large amounts showcase whiskey's unique flavor and shouldn't be substituted. The major whiskey-producing countries are Scotland and Canada, where it's whisky without the "e," along with Ireland and the United States.

American	Made from rye, also known as Rye Whiskey
Bourbon	Made from corn, must originate in Bourbon county, Kentucky
Canadian whisky	Made from potatoes, a blended whisky aged 4 years in oak, production supervised by the Canadian government
Irish whiskey	Made from barley, blended, smoky taste
Rye	Made from rye
Scotch	Made from barley, a blended whisky, originates in Scotland
Tennessee whiskey	Made from corn, originates in Tennessee

Wine

Wine has been made from fermented grapes since ancient times throughout the world. The type of grape used produces different colors and flavors. When baking with wine, there are several categories to be aware of:

Still Wine	Uncarbonated, red, white, or rosé, can be dry or sweet
Sparkling Wine	Effervescent/carbonated, like Champagne or Asti Spumante
Fortified Wines	Brandy, sherry, port, or other spirits added
Aromatic Wines	Flavored with herbs and spices, e.g., vermouth

How Much Alcohol Stays in My Baking?*

When alcohol is stirred into the batter and baked:

Baking time	Alcohol retained
15 minutes	40 percent
30 minutes	35 percent
1 hour	25 percent

When alcohol is put on top of batter and then baked:

Baking time	Alcohol retained
25 minutes	45 percent

When alcohol is soaked into cakes after baking:

Method	Alcohol retained
No heat, stored overnight	70 percent

When alcohol is added to frostings, creams, and flambé:

Method	Alcohol retained
Stirred in, no heat	100 percent
Added to boiling liquid	85 percent
Flamed	75 percent

*Source: U.S. Department of Agriculture's Nutrient Data Laboratory Study

The Booze Cake Rating System

We've ranked the confections you'll find in this book by type of cake, occasion, and—most importantly—the Booze Meter.

Type of Cake

Layer cake	2-layer cake	3-layer cake	Tube cake
Sheet cake	Loaf cake	Bundt cake	Cupcakes
Shortcakes	Tea cakes	Bite-size pieces	Glass/punch bowl cake

Occasion

Dinner parties	Special occasions	Big parties
Birthdays	Romantic occasions	Sports parties
Brunch	Barbeques and picnics	Winter holidays

The Booze Meter

Lightweight	Feeling it	Totally tipsy

Please Bake Responsibly

The conventional wisdom is that booze simply evaporates in the oven. That's simply not true. The amount of intoxicant that remains in cake depends on the baking time. In the oven, alcohol's harshness quickly evaporates, leaving a deep, rich flavor and residual alcoholic content.

Most recipes in this book contain between 1 tablespoon and ½ cup of alcohol—not a tremendous amount, but a big flavor enhancement. Some cakes are subtly flavored; others are downright intoxicating. Each cake's Booze Meter is a helpful guide to how much alcohol stays in the cake.

It's possible that the amount of alcohol in these cakes *could* get someone drunk, but it most likely won't. However, be sure to let nibblers know that these baked goods contain booze. Be considerate of teetotalers and those with alcohol sensitivities or abuse issues. And, as fun as it is to joke about the joys of baking and drinking, please don't operate kitchen equipment while intoxicated! Friends don't let friends bake drunk.

Garnishing Cocktails & Cakes

Garnishes dress up a cocktail like toppings dress up cakes. To hardcore bartenders, there is a perfect garnish for every drink: a cherry is used in a Manhattan, fresh mint sprigs for mint juleps, and a pineapple wedge and maraschino cherry for piña coladas. Many of these flavor-enhancing extras can be used for cakes as well. So in addition to traditional cake toppers, we suggest using drink garnishes to decorate your booze cakes. Some garnishes commonly used on both beverages and baked goods are:

- Shaved or curled chocolate
- Shredded coconut
- Whipped cream
- Peppermints
- Nonpareils or sprinkles
- Nutmeg

It's also fun to play with cocktail picks and swizzle sticks, which are available in loads of adorable themes and a variety of shapes and sizes. There are no rules when it comes to Booze Cakes, so have fun! Here are some suggestions.

Citrus

Lemon, lime, and orange zest garnishes, or citrus fruit peels, are simple yet versatile. Use a microplane or zester and be sure to include only the colored part, not the pith.

- Twist and knot the zests
- Make slits in slices to create borders on cake edges
- Notch the zest to make grooves and patterns
- Twist slices around a skewer, combine with other fruits
- Cut shapes (circles, stars, butterflies, etc.) from the peel using cookie cutters
- Cut long spirals from the zest

14

Berries & Cherries	Berries and cherries can be used in a variety of ways:

Berries & Cherries

Berries and cherries can be used in a variety of ways:
- Buy Maraschino cocktail cherries in different colors
- Skewer a trio of cherries or alternating berries and cherries
- Add stemmed maraschino cherries
- Decorate with sliced or candied strawberries
- Remove the top of a whole strawberry and replace with a mint leaf

Flavored Sugars

Flavored sugars are used by bartenders to rim glasses, but for cakes you can:
- Randomly sprinkle them on top
- Form patterns freehand or with a stencil

Miscellaneous Fruit

Miscellaneous fruit with peels can be fun:
- Cut a kumquat peel and make it into flowers
- Slice kiwi and shape the peel
- Cut apples into slices and wedges; leave the peel on to show color
- Cut a hole in an apple slice and insert a cherry or berry

Tropical Fruits

Tropical fruits are a classic cocktail garnish:
- Slice papaya, melon, fresh coconut, and pineapple into wedges
- Scoop out watermelon, cantaloupe, and honeydew melon, alternating slices on a skewer
- Alternate starfruit and lychees
- Dip banana in lemon to prevent discoloration; sprinkle with spice

Flowers & Herbs

Flowers and herbs are unexpected and create a fresh and beautiful presentation. Some edible varieties include:
- Orchids (for tropical-inspired cakes)
- Roses or rose petals (the white part of the petal may be slightly bitter)
- Sprigs of mint, chamomile
- Candied pansies or violets (page 136)

Seven Tips for Success

One thing that stops people from baking is fear. They're afraid that they can't do it right, or that their confections won't turn out properly. Or they are afraid that baking is too expensive, that their tools aren't right, or that they can't locate special baking ingredients. To this we say: Don't let fear stand in the way of fun! There are two types of bakers, those who are perfectionists and those who are more improvisational. We fall into the second category. We'll fuss if it's worth the time and effort, but we're busy people, and more often than not we just want reliably good cakes without a lot of hassle. Here are some things we've discovered that make our baking a success time and time again.

1. **Keep a Baking Pantry** You never know when the mood will strike you to bake, right? Sure, sometimes you have a special occasion and things need to be done just right, so that's the time to go shopping for the perfect ingredients. Other times you just want to get messy in the kitchen or sweeten your mood with a treat. That's why it's a good idea to keep baking basics on hand in your pantry: flour, sugar, butter, cocoa, eggs, and vanilla. We keep our bars stocked with the basics too: vodka, brandy, rum, and few key liqueurs. Come over to our house at any time, and we can bake a cake or make a cocktail or combine them both into a boozy cake. We're ready.

2. **Read the Whole Recipe** Seriously, read it all the way through before you begin. It may sound obvious, but you'd be surprised how often people don't read the entire recipe first, and then run into all sorts of difficulty.

3. **Tools and Ingredients Do Matter** Sure, you can wing it. When we do it, we call it improvisation. We're designers by profession, so we're used to creating by a variety of means. However, over the years we've found that a few good tools are worth investing in. You'll love them and use them for years. Using fresh ingredients is important as well. Old stuff just doesn't always do what it's supposed to do. We've found that sometimes the right ingredients can make or break a cake. Then again, if you're willing to roll with it, as we are most of the time, you can find interesting new recipe variations by substituting ingredients that you have on hand. In fact, that's why you'll see many variations of our recipes in this book.

4. **Prep Makes Baking Easy** Get ready to bake by assembling everything you'll need within reach. Pull out the equipment, prep the pans, preheat your oven, measure out ingredients and prepare them for use—for example, separate the eggs, soften the butter, zest the citrus, chop the nuts, whatever—so you can move easily from one step to the next. The more thorough we are in the beginning, the more efficient we are once we're baking. Smart prep work makes the baking process much smoother and means that the cocktail drinking can commence much sooner.

5.   **Allow Space and Time to Bake** Give yourself permission to make a mess. Spread out. Use your whole kitchen. And don't rush through your baking. Think of it as "me time," not another chore on your to-do list. Sure, there are instances when you just want the baking done and the sweet stuff in your stomach. We get it. Making a cake from scratch is going to take more than a minute to accomplish, but it doesn't have to be a big ordeal. Check out the tipsy Harvey Wallbanger (pages 56 to 57) if you need a quick cake fix.

6.   **Practice, Practice, Practice** Your skills improve and expand with each cake you bake. We encourage you to make notes and document your experiences: It will inform how you make the same recipe the next time around. Try different techniques, tools, and ingredients. See how you like them. Develop your own versions of the booze cakes you bake. Increase or reduce the amount of booze in your cakes. Remember: The great thing about baking practice is that you get to eat your mistakes!

7.   **Relax and Have Fun** Cake is not vital to life. OK, scratch that, it is to some people. What we mean is that no one is ever going to die from a badly frosted cake that is totally lopsided. If that were true, all of our close friends would've been goners by now. We think it's fun to play in the kitchen and then eat the results. Sometimes we make cake wrecks. Sometimes we surprise ourselves with our superior skills and gorgeous pro-style cakes. But we always enjoy the process. If it all gets to be too much, kick back, pour yourself a drink, and start again another day.

1 Classic Booze Cakes
RECIPES THAT TRADITIONALLY CONTAIN ALCOHOL

Spiked confections have been around since the days of the Roman army, when commanders laced fruitcake with alcohol to keep soldiers happy on long journeys. But most traditional booze cakes were dreamed up to celebrate holidays and holy days. Whether it's a rich and creamy Tipsy Tiramisu for a special birthday, a Pink Champagne Cake for a bachelorette party, or some enchanted Black Forest Cupcakes for the holidays, these traditional treats will sweeten your entertaining in scrumptious style.

Bananas Foster Gingerbread Flambé

TYPE OF CAKE	SERVINGS	BAKING TIME	BOOZE METER	OCCASION
🧁	10 to 12	20 to 25	☺	🍽 ♡

Spiked Banana Gingerbread Cupcakes
1 (3-inch) piece fresh ginger
¾ cup ripe banana, mashed
¼ cup cognac
6 tablespoons (¾ stick) unsalted butter
⅓ cup blackstrap molasses
¾ cup dark brown sugar
1 egg
2 cups all-purpose flour
2 teaspoons baking powder
½ teaspoon baking soda
½ teaspoon salt
2 teaspoons ground ginger
1 teaspoon ground cinnamon
¾ teaspoon nutmeg

Foster Sauce
¾ cup dark brown sugar
6 tablespoons (¾ stick) unsalted butter
3 tablespoons light corn syrup
3 tablespoons cognac
3 tablespoons crème de banana

Finishing
4 bananas, sliced lengthwise
Vanilla ice cream for serving

THIS FLAMING NEW ORLEANS DESSERT was all the rage in the 1950s. Bananas were new to the American palate, so flaming, booze-drenched bananas served over ice cream were exotic and decadent. Turn off the lights, soften the jazz, and ignite this flambé cake. It will be a spectacularly memorable performance.

Prepare

1. Preheat oven to 350°F. Grease two cupcake pans.

Make

2. In a saucepan, bring ginger and ½ cup water to a boil. Remove from heat and let steep 15 minutes; discard ginger. Stir mashed banana and cognac into the ginger water.
3. In a mixing bowl, beat butter, molasses, and brown sugar until creamy. Beat in egg. In a separate bowl, sift together flour, baking powder, baking soda, salt, ginger, cinnamon, and nutmeg. Beat the flour and banana-ginger-cognac mixtures into the butter mixture in three alternating additions. Pour into pans and bake 20 to 25 minutes or until golden brown.
4. For the sauce: In a saucepan over medium heat, combine brown sugar, butter, and corn syrup. Stir until contents reach a low simmer. Remove from heat and stir in cognac and crème de banana.

Finish

5. Heat a flambé pan in a warm oven (275°F) 10 to 15 minutes. Remove and place on a hotplate in the center of the table. Arrange sliced

Banana Nut Gingerbread Flambé
For the cake: Add 1 cup nuts to the batter. For the sauce: Mix in ⅓ cup nuts along with cognac and crème de banana.

Cranberry Banana Gingerbread Flambé
For the cake: Add 1 cup whole cranberries to the batter. For the sauce: Replace crème de banana with cranberry liqueur.

bananas around the perimeter of pan and add a few spoonfuls of sauce. Stack the cupcakes in the center. Top with ice cream and remaining sauce and ignite. Be prepared for "oohs!" and "aahs!" but don't get distracted. You don't want to torch yourself, your guests, or your home.

FLAMBÉ IT!

A flaming cake is a tasty, caramelized treat. When lit, alcohol vapor burns with a cool blue flame, lessening the liquor's alcohol content but leaving its rich, sugary flavors. The secret to flambé is that both the liquor and the cake must be warm. Brandy, cognac, rum, Grand Marnier, Cointreau, and Chambord are all excellent for flaming. Eighty-proof liquors are best. A word of warning: Those above 120-proof are highly flammable and dangerous. The alcohol content of wine, beer, and Champagne is typically too low to ignite.

Safety Tips:
- Do not ignite over an open flame, use a hotplate instead
- Use long fireplace matches or propane barbecue lighter
- Tie up long hair, roll up sleeves, and stand back
- Wear a flameproof oven mitt
- Use a special metal flambé or deep-dish pan
- Keep a pan lid nearby to extinguish out-of-control flames
- Do not pour alcohol over flames

Black Forest Cupcakes

TYPE OF CAKE	SERVINGS	BAKING TIME	BOOZE METER	OCCASION
🧁	⑱	⏰ 20	☺	♡ 🥂

Chocolate Liqueur Pudding
1 (3.8-ounce) box instant devil's food pudding mix
1 cup milk
¼ cup vodka

Chocolate Cherry Cupcakes
½ cup unsweetened cocoa powder
3 ounce bittersweet chocolate, chopped
¾ cup (1½ sticks) unsalted butter
1½ cups sugar
4 eggs
1 teaspoon vanilla extract
1 teaspoon kirsch
1 tablespoon cherry liqueur
1 tablespoon chocolate liqueur
2 cups all-purpose flour
1 teaspoon baking soda
¼ teaspoon salt
1 cup sour cream

Black Cherry Compote
Juice of 1 lime
¾ cup sugar
2 cups frozen sweet cherries
2 teaspoons cornstarch
¼ cup kirsch

Cherry Whipped Cream
1¼ cups heavy cream
1 cup confectioners' sugar
1 teaspoon kirsch

Finishing
24 maraschino cherries

HANSEL AND GRETEL, Little Red Riding Hood, Snow White and the Seven Dwarfs, Goldilocks and the Three Bears—all these fairy tales start when hungry travelers encounter adventures in the deep dark woods. The Black Forest region of Germany is the mysterious home to many of these enchanting tales as well as the equally delightful *Schwarzwälder kirschtorte*, better known as Black Forest cake. Its dark chocolate, sour cherry, and kirsch liqueur flavors make for magical cupcakes.

Prepare

1. Preheat oven to 350°F. Grease two 12-cup cupcake pans.

Make

2. For the pudding: In a mixing bowl, whisk pudding mix, milk, and vodka until mixture thickens, about 2 minutes. Chill 1 hour in refrigerator.
3. For the cupcakes: Dissolve cocoa powder in ⅔ cup boiling water. Stir in bittersweet chocolate until melted and smooth. Set aside to cool.
4. In a mixing bowl, cream butter and sugar 3 to 5 minutes or until light and fluffy. Add the eggs one at a time, beating after each addition. Stir in vanilla, kirsch, and both liqueurs.
5. In a separate bowl, combine flour, baking soda, and salt. Slowly mix flour mixture and sour cream into the butter mixture. Stir in cooled melted chocolate. Pour into pans and bake 20 minutes, or until a toothpick inserted in the center of a cupcake comes out clean.
6. For the compote: In a saucepan, bring lime juice and sugar to a boil. Reduce to a simmer and add cherries. Cook 10 minutes, stirring occasionally. Stir in cornstarch and kirsch. Reduce to a simmer and stir occasionally until thickened, about 5 minutes, being careful not to overcook so the cherries stay plump.

Three-layer Black Forest Cake
For the cake: Double the chocolate kirsch sour-cream cake recipe and bake in three 10-inch cake pans 35 to 40 minutes. Once cooled, place the bottom layer on a cake plate. For the finishing: Top with half black cherry compote and half chocolate liqueur pudding. Add the second layer and repeat. Add the top layer and decorate with cherry whipped cream and maraschino or chocolate-covered cherries.

Black Forest Cupcakes with Chocolate-Covered Cherries
For the finishing: Top cupcakes (or cake) with rich, kirsch liqueur-filled chocolate-covered cherries (store-bought or homemade, page 138).

7. **For the whipped cream:** In a mixing bowl, whip all ingredients until soft peaks form. Refrigerate until ready to serve.

Finish

8. Cut the cupcakes in half horizontally. Spoon dollops of black cherry compote and/or chocolate liqueur pudding over the cupcake bottoms. Replace the tops and garnish with another dollop of pudding, some cherry whipped cream, and a maraschino cherry.

A WINTER WONDERLAND COCKTAIL

The Black Forest cocktail is rich and delicious—a liquid version of Black Forest cake!

Black Forest Cocktail
2 ounces crème de cacao
2 ounces cherry liqueur
2 ounces kirsch
2 ounces cream

Combine the crème de cacao, cherry liqueur, kirsch, and cream over ice and garnish with whipped cream, chocolate shavings, and a maraschino cherry. Or add a Block Forest cocktail to a mug of steaming hot chocolate for a delicious winter warm-up.

English Trifle

Buttermilk Brandy Shortcake

2 cups all-purpose flour

¼ cup sugar

3 teaspoons baking powder

½ teaspoon salt

5½ tablespoons unsalted butter

¾ cup buttermilk

2 eggs, beaten

1 teaspoon vanilla extract

3 tablespoons brandy

Three-Berry Filling

1 cup strawberries, sliced

1 cup raspberries

1 cup blueberries

¾ cup sugar

½ cup lemon juice

Brandy Cream

2 cups heavy cream

3 tablespoons confectioners' sugar

2 tablespoons brandy

ANYTIME YOU PUT CAKE, fresh berries, and whipped cream together, the results are bound to be delicious. English trifle is more a method than a recipe: It's made by combining layers of cake and fruit with cream or custard. Some recipes call for spirits; this one includes brandy and an easy baking method similar to that of biscuits rather than classic shortcake.

Prepare

1. Preheat oven to 400°F. Grease and flour one 9-by-13-inch cake pan or shortcake pan.

Make

2. In a bowl, combine flour, sugar, baking powder, and salt. Cut in butter until mixture is crumbly. In a separate bowl, stir together buttermilk, eggs, vanilla, and brandy. Make a well in the center of the flour mixture and, all at once, pour in the buttermilk mixture. Mix together with a fork (or fingers) until just moistened. The batter will be lumpy.
3. Spread evenly in the pan. Bake 10 to 15 minutes, or until a knife inserted in the center comes out clean. Place shortcake on a rack and allow to cool completely before cutting it into three equal portions.
4. For the filling: Combine all ingredients in a medium bowl.
5. For the cream: In a mixing bowl, beat cream and sugar on high speed. Add brandy and beat until fluffy. Refrigerate while cake cools.

Finish

6. To assemble, layer pieces of cake in individual serving glasses or one large serving bowl (a glass loaf pan is perfect) and spread a

ENGLISH TRIFLE

Peach Trifle

For the cake, fruit filling, and cream: Substitute peaches for berries and rum for brandy.

Sherry Trifle

For the cake, fruit filling, and cream: Replace brandy with sherry.

Traditional Trifle

For the cake, fruit filling, and cream: Layer ladyfingers (page 45), berries, and cream in a glass bowl (traditionally with a pedestal).

large spoonful of brandy cream overtop. Spread a third of the berry filling evenly on top of the cream. Repeat for middle and top layers. Finish with a dollop of cream and a few more berries.

BRANDY COCKTAILS

Brandy is the alcohol distilled from fermented fruit juices, including wine. Derived from the Dutch word *brandewijn*, meaning "burnt wine," brandy may be distilled from any fruit. Measuring in at around 80 proof, grape-derived brandies include cognac, Armagnac, grappa, and Jerez. Other fruit brandies derive their flavors from the fruit from which they are made, including apple, cherry, peach, and so on. Unlike other cocktails that require the best of spirits, you should never waste a fine cognac in a brandy drink—drink it straight.

Brandy Alexander

1 ounce brandy
1 ounce crème de cacao
1 ounce heavy cream
Pinch of nutmeg, freshly grated

Shake the brandy, crème de cacao, and cream with ice; then strain into a chilled cocktail glass. Garnish with a pinch of nutmeg and always serve with cake or cookies.

Scorpion

1 ounce brandy
1 ounce light rum
3 ounces unsweetened pineapple juice
½ ounce orgeat
Dash of grenadine

Shake all ingredients with ice; then strain over ice into a chilled highball glass.

Golden Rum Cake

TYPE OF CAKE	SERVINGS	BAKING TIME	BOOZE METER	OCCASION
🍮	⑩	⏰ 60	😃	🥂 ❄

Golden Rum Cake
1 cup (2 sticks) unsalted butter
2 cups sugar
4 eggs
3 cups all-purpose flour
1 teaspoon baking powder
½ teaspoon baking soda
⅛ teaspoon salt
1 cup milk
1 teaspoon vanilla extract
¾ cup dark rum

Golden Rum Glaze
4 tablespoons (½ stick) unsalted butter
1 cup sugar
½ cup dark rum

Finishing
3 tablespoons confectioners' sugar

Variations

Chocolate Rum Cake
For the sauce: Substitute spiked chocolate sauce (page 59).

Nutty Golden Rum Cake
For the cake: Add ½ cup chopped pecans to batter. For the finishing: After glazing, top with candied nuts or brittle.

Spiced Golden Rum Cake
For the cake and glaze: Substitute spiced rum for dark rum. Add ½ teaspoon cinnamon and ½ teaspoon nutmeg to flour in step 3.

DURING THE WINTER HOLIDAYS, magazines abound with recipes for golden rum cakes that call for packaged cake mix and instant pudding (similar to the Harvey Wallbanger Cake on pages 56 to 57). You can choose to go that route and glaze a box-mix cake, or you can whip this one up from scratch. Either way, the more rum you add, the more this little wonder absorbs it—and the more holiday cheer gets passed around!

Prepare

1. Preheat oven to 350°F. Grease and flour a 9- or 10-inch Bundt or tube cake pan.

Make

2. In a mixing bowl, cream butter and sugar until light and fluffy. Add eggs one at a time, beating after each addition.
3. Combine flour, baking powder, baking soda, and salt. In another bowl, combine milk, vanilla, and rum. Beat flour mixture and milk mixture into butter in three alternating additions. Pour batter into the prepared pan. Bake 1 hour, or until golden brown.

Finish

4. For the glaze: Melt butter in a saucepan over low heat. Stir in sugar and ¼ cup water and bring to a boil; cook 5 minutes, stirring constantly. Remove from heat and stir in rum.
5. Place cake on a serving platter. Slowly pour glaze over top and sides until completely absorbed. Dust with confectioners' sugar.

Honey Spice Beer Cake

TYPE OF CAKE	SERVINGS	BAKING TIME	BOOZE METER	OCCASION
⬭	(10) to (12)	(40) to (45)	☺	⚇ ⚥

Honey Spice Beer Cake
3¾ cups all-purpose flour
1 teaspoon baking soda
2 teaspoons baking powder
¼ teaspoon salt
1 teaspoon cloves
1 teaspoon cinnamon
1 teaspoon allspice
1 teaspoon nutmeg
½ cup (1 stick) salted butter
1 cup light brown sugar
1 cup sugar
4 eggs
1¼ cup honey
Juice and grated zest of 1 lemon
1 (12-ounce) bottle honey beer

Honey Beer Frosting
½ cup (1 stick) salted butter
3½ cups confectioners' sugar
½ cup honey beer
2 tablespoons honey

Finishing
2 cups mixed nuts

SEVEN THOUSAND YEARS AGO, people in the region of what is present-day Iran brewed yeast into the first alcoholic drinks, inventing what we now know as beer. Unfortunately, they had no cake. The ancient Egyptians also drank beer, and although they used yeast to make the first cakes sweetened with honey, they didn't think to combine beer and cake to make one of humanity's greatest inventions: beer cake. For this tremendous recipe you can try lager, Guinness, or your favorite brew; each one imparts a different flavor.

Prepare

1. Preheat oven to 325°F. Grease and flour a 9-by-13-inch sheet-cake pan.

Make

2. Combine flour, baking soda, baking powder, salt, cloves, cinnamon, allspice, and nutmeg; set aside. In a mixing bowl, cream butter and sugars 3 to 5 minutes, or until light and fluffy. Add eggs one at a time, beating after each addition. Mix in honey, lemon juice, and zest.
3. Mix in flour mixture and beer in three alternating additions. Bake 40 to 45 minutes, or until a knife comes out clean. Remove from oven and cool.
4. For the frosting: In a mixing bowl, cream butter with about one-third of the confectioners' sugar. Mix in beer and the rest of the sugar in alternating additions, beating until smooth and creamy. Stir in honey.

Finish

5. Remove cake from the pan and place on a plate large enough to hold the cake and nuts. Cover with frosting and scatter nuts on top and around the plate.

Variations

Beer Pound Cake
For the cake: Omit cloves, cinnamon, allspice, and nutmeg from the batter. Use your favorite beer instead of honey beer.

Devil's Food Beer Cake
For the cake: Reduce flour to 3 cups; omit cloves, cinnamon, allspice, and nutmeg; and add 1 cup Dutch-processed cocoa and 1 cup chocolate chips. For the frosting: Replace honey with ½ cup Dutch-processed cocoa.

Devil's Food Spice Beer Cake
For the cake: Reduce flour to 3 cups. Add 1 cup Dutch-processed cocoa and 1 cup chocolate chips. For the frosting: Add ½ cup Dutch-processed cocoa and omit honey.

Stout Black Walnut Cake
For the cake and frosting: Replace honey beer with Stout. Stir 1½ cups toasted walnuts into the cake batter.

BEER COCKTAILS

Any beer mixed with practically anything qualifies as a beer cocktail. However, some taste better than others. Here are a few of the more palatable varieties, perfect for pairing with beer cakes, as well as pretzels, mixed nuts, and other bar snacks.

Beer Buster
1½ ounces vodka, chilled
2 dashes of Tabasco
1 (12-ounce) bottle of beer

Stir the vodka and Tobasco in a chilled mug; then add the beer.

Black Velvet
6 ounces Guinness, cold
6 ounces Champagne, cold

Pour Guinness and Champagne into a beer glass, but do not stir.

Boilermaker Pour a shot of scotch into a mug of beer. Dropping the shot glass into the mug makes it a Depth Charge.

Skip and Go Naked Mix together however much beer, gin, grenadine, and lemon juice you have. Drink this American frat house classic at your own risk.

Jamaican Ginger Cakes with Vanilla Butter Rum Sauce

TYPE OF CAKE	SERVINGS	BAKING TIME	BOOZE METER	OCCASION
🧁 or 🍰🎂	(12)	(20) to (25)	☺	🌅 🎁

Ginger Cakes

½ cup (1 stick) unsalted butter
¾ cups brown sugar
2 eggs
2 tablespoons ginger, freshly grated
½ teaspoon vanilla extract
¼ cup dark rum
1¾ cups all-purpose flour
1½ teaspoons ground ginger
1½ teaspoon baking powder
⅛ teaspoon salt
⅓ cup buttermilk

Vanilla Butter Rum Sauce

½ cup (1 stick) unsalted butter, melted
½ cup sugar
¼ cup honey
¼ cup evaporated milk
¼ cup light rum
2 teaspoons vanilla extract

Finishing

½ cup candied ginger, chopped
Vanilla or rum-raisin ice cream to serve

Variation

Jamaican Ginger Cakes with Candied Rum Ginger

For the finishing: It's easy to candy your own fresh ginger—and add a taste of rum in the process! (See page 137 for directions.)

FRESH GINGER AND JAMAICAN RUM are a killer combination! This recipe was inspired by the homey Jamaican ginger *bulla* (the Jamaican word for "cake"). We love to serve these gingery cakes with homemade gingersnaps (pages 139 to 140) and a scoop of rum-raisin ice cream drizzled with warm, gooey vanilla-butter-rum sauce.

Prepare

1. Preheat oven to 350°F. Grease a 12-cup cupcake pan or individual cake molds.

Make

2. In a mixing bowl, cream butter and sugar 3 to 5 minutes, or until light and fluffy. Beat in eggs one at a time. Stir in ginger, vanilla, and rum. Sift together flour, ground ginger, baking powder, and salt. Add flour mixture and buttermilk to the creamed butter mixture in three alternating additions. Bake 20 to 25 minutes, or until a knife inserted in the center comes out clean.

3. For the sauce: In a saucepan over medium heat, bring butter, sugar, honey, and evaporated milk to a boil. Lower to a simmer, add rum and vanilla, and cook 1 to 2 minutes.

Finish

4. Put cakes into serving bowls. Add a generous scoop of vanilla or rum-raisin ice cream, and sprinkle with candied ginger. Pour hot vanilla butter rum sauce overtop.

Lane Cake

TYPE OF CAKE	SERVINGS	BAKING TIME	BOOZE METER	OCCASION
🎂	(10)	(30) *to* (35)	☺	🪑 🥂 👯

White Cake

1 cup (2 sticks) unsalted butter

2 cups sugar

1 teaspoon vanilla extract

2 tablespoons bourbon

4 cups all-purpose flour

1 tablespoon baking powder

½ teaspoon salt

¾ cup whole milk

10 egg whites (reserve yolks for the filling)

Fruit-and-Coconut Filling

¾ cup (1½ sticks) unsalted butter

1¾ cups sugar

⅓ teaspoon salt

10 egg yolks

2 cups pecans, toasted, then chopped

1 cup golden raisins, chopped

1½ cups assorted dried fruits, chopped

½ cup candied cherries

1½ cups unsweetened shredded coconut, toasted

1 cup bourbon

⅓ cup orange juice

Bourbon Buttercream

1 cup (2 sticks) unsalted butter

¼ teaspoon salt

3 cups confectioners' sugar

¼ cup bourbon

¼ cup half-and-half

THIS WHITE LAYER CAKE spiked with bourbon is a Southern U.S. specialty. Mrs. Emma Rylander Lane's version won prizes at the 1898 Alabama and Georgia county fairs, and ever since it's been called Lane Cake, Alabama Lane cake, or prize cake. You can frost the entire cake with bourbon buttercream or spread the fruit-and-coconut filling on top and the bourbon buttercream on the sides. Bourbon is traditionally added to the frosting; we've added it to the frosting *and* the cake.

Prepare

1. Preheat oven to 325°F. Grease and flour three 8-inch cake pans.

Make

2. In a mixing bowl, cream butter and sugar 3 to 5 minutes, or until light and fluffy. Stir in vanilla and bourbon. In a bowl, combine flour, baking powder, and salt. Add flour mixture and milk to the butter mixture in three alternating additions; start and stop with the flour to prevent curdling.

3. In a mixing bowl, beat egg whites to soft peaks. Gently fold egg whites into the batter. Pour batter into the prepared pans and bake 30 to 35 minutes, or until the cakes are golden and a knife inserted into the center comes out clean. Let cool completely.

4. For the filling: Melt butter in a deep saucepan over medium heat. Remove from heat and whisk in sugar, salt, and egg yolks. Return to medium heat, stirring constantly with a wooden spoon until it begins to thicken and a candy thermometer reads 180°F. Remove from heat and stir in the nuts, raisins, dried fruits, candied cherries, coconut, bourbon, and orange juice. Allow filling to cool.

5. For the buttercream: In a mixing bowl, beat butter and salt until creamy. Add confectioners' sugar and bourbon in alternating

Whiskey Lane Cake
For the cake, filling, and buttercream: Substitute rye or sour-mash whiskey for bourbon.

Six-Layer Lane Cake
For the finishing: Cut each layer cake in half lengthwise for an elegant six-layer cake.

additions. Slowly add half and half and continue beating until fluffy. Refrigerate until ready to use.

Finish

6. Place one layer on a cake plate and spread half the filling almost to the outer rim with a spatula. Place the next layer on top and add the remaining filling. Add the final layer.
7. With a clean spatula, spread the bourbon buttercream on the sides and top of the cake. This cake benefits from sitting a few hours so all the flavors can meld.

THE LANE CAKE IN LITERATURE

This classic Southern cake is the dessert of choice in Alabama-native Harper Lee's prize-winning novel, *To Kill a Mockingbird*. It's baked to welcome guests, celebrate festive occasions, and say thank you—or to create a welcome distraction.

Jem and Scout Finch's neighbor Miss Maudie Atkinson's Lane Cakes are known as "the best cakes in the neighborhood." When Miss Maudie's house burns down, she surprises Scout by somehow still having the time and wherewithal to bake a lovely Lane cake to thank their neighbor Mr. Avery for fighting the fire. When Aunt Alexandra Hancock arrives to stay with the Finches, Miss Maudie makes a particularly boozy Lane cake to honor her arrival. Noting the cake's alcoholic kick, Scout says, "Miss Maudie baked a Lane Cake so loaded with shinny it made me tight." In the 1930s in the South, "shinny" was a slang term for liquor and "tight" was (and is still) a slang term for drunk. Bake a shinny Lane cake any time you want to get good and tight!

Pink Champagne Cake

TYPE OF CAKE	SERVINGS	BAKING TIME	BOOZE METER	OCCASION
🍰	⑩ to ⑫	⏰ 35	☺	🎁 ♡ 🥂

Pink Champagne Cake

3 cups all-purpose flour

3 teaspoons baking powder

½ teaspoon salt

1 cup (2 sticks) unsalted butter

2 cups sugar

1 teaspoon vanilla extract

6 egg whites

A few drops red food coloring

2 cups Champagne

Pink Champagne Frosting

¾ cup (1½ sticks) unsalted butter

4 cups confectioners' sugar

½ cup Champagne

¼ cup whole milk

1 tablespoon vanilla extract

A few drops red food coloring

TRADITIONALLY, a Champagne Cake is a white cake layered with rum, Bavarian or whipped cream filling, pink buttercream icing—and not an ounce of Champagne! This recipe lightens the crumb by including a splash of bubbly. It can also be made into a chocolate champagne cake or a fluffy white champagne cake (page 41). Any way you slice it, it's a light dessert perfect for Valentine's Day, anniversaries, and especially New Year's Eve.

Prepare

1. Preheat oven to 350°F. Grease and flour two 9-inch round cake pans.

Make

2. In a bowl, combine flour, baking powder, and salt; set aside. In a mixing bowl, beat butter and sugar 3 to 5 minutes, or until light and fluffy. Add vanilla and beat in egg whites one at a time.

3. Mix in food coloring. Beat in flour mixture and Champagne in three alternating additions, starting and ending with flour to prevent curdling. Pour batter into pans and bake 35 minutes, or until a knife inserted in the center comes out clean.

4. For the frosting: In a mixing bowl, beat butter 1 minute. Gradually add the confectioners' sugar, Champagne, milk, vanilla, and food coloring; beat until smooth and creamy.

Finish

5. Once cake has cooled completely, place bottom layer on a cake plate and spread half the frosting overtop. Add top layer and cover with frosting.

Chocolate Champagne Cake

For the cake: Reduce flour to 2½ cups and add ¾ cup Dutch-processed cocoa. Reduce confectioners' sugar to 3½ cups and add ½ cup cocoa. Omit food coloring. For the frosting: Omit food coloring.

White Champagne Cake

For the cake: Omit food coloring. For the frosting: Omit food coloring. Top with white chocolate curls.

THE CHAMPAGNE COCKTAIL

The Champagne cocktail is a marvelously simple mixture of Champagne and a sugar cube soaked in Angostura bitters. This classic cocktail dates back to the Civil War era in the United States, when it appeared in *Jerry Thomas' Bartenders Guide: How to Mix Drinks, or, The Bon-Vivant's Companion*. The Champagne cocktail was chosen by *Esquire* magazine as one of the top ten cocktails of 1934; although its popularity has waned, it still has unflagging adherents. For some sophisticates, it is still the only cocktail.

For a Champagne cake or Champagne cocktail, there's no need to purchase a pricey bottle of bubbly. The addition of sugar nicely rounds out a less expensive brand.

Champagne Cocktail

1 dash of Angostura bitters
1 sugar cube
Dry Champagne, chilled
Twist of lemon peel

Add the dash of bitters to the sugar cube in the bottom of a chilled Champagne glass, and slowly pour in the Champagne. Garnish with lemon twist.

Champagne Normande Add 1 teaspoon of Calvados to the basic Champagne cocktail.

Mimosa Pour 2 ounces fresh orange juice into a chilled Champagne glass, and slowly add 4 ounces of Champagne.

Sweet & Salty Nut-Roll Torte

TYPE OF CAKE	SERVINGS	BAKING TIME	BOOZE METER	OCCASION
🍰	⑩	⏰60 + ⏰30	☺	🍴🍽🍴 🥂

Golden Walnut Cake
4 eggs, separated
½ cup walnuts, ground fine
½ cup sugar
½ cup all-purpose flour
2 teaspoons baking powder

Sweet & Salty Nut Filling
2 cups walnuts, chopped
1 (10-ounce) container salted mixed
   nuts, chopped
¼ cup sugar
¼ cup brown sugar
½ cup (1 stick) unsalted butter, melted
2 eggs, beaten
2 tablespoons spiced rum

Rum Honey
¼ cup honey
¼ cup spiced rum

Finish
Toasted meringues, store-bought or
   homemade (page 140)

Variations

Apple Raisin Nut-Roll Torte
For the filling: Reduce nuts by
1 cup; add ¾ cup chopped apples
and ¼ cup raisins.

Chocolate Nut-Roll Torte
For the sauce: Substitute spiked chocolate sauce (page 59) for rum honey.

EASTERN EUROPEANS MAKE a classic salty-sweet confection called a nut roll in English, or *bejgli* in Hungarian, *potica* in Slovenian, *makowiec* in Polish, and *orechovnik* in Slovak, among other names. It's a yeast sweetbread filled with a combination of nuts or fruit and usually rolled like a jellyroll or pinwheel. Thin layers of golden walnut cake are lavished with rum honey and mixed nuts and then topped with toasted walnut meringues.

Prepare

1. Preheat oven to 375°F. Grease and flour a 9-by-13-inch cake pan.

Make

2. In a mixing bowl, beat egg whites until stiff. Gently fold in walnuts; set aside. In a mixing bowl, beat egg yolks and sugar until light and thick. Beat in flour and baking powder and gently fold in whipped egg whites. Pour into the pan and bake 30 minutes, or until golden brown. Allow to cool completely.
3. For the filling: In a saucepan over medium heat, combine nuts, sugars, melted butter, eggs, and rum. Stir to combine. Cook 20 minutes, stirring occasionally.
4. For the rum honey: Microwave honey and spiced rum 1 to 2 minutes; stir to combine.

Finish

5. Cut cake into three equal pieces. Place one layer on a serving plate and pour rum honey overtop. Add a layer of filling. Repeat for middle layer; place last layer on top. Top with rum honey and meringues.

Tipsy Tiramisu

TYPE OF CAKE	SERVINGS	BAKING TIME	BOOZE METER	OCCASION
🍮	⑥	⏰10	☺	🍴🍽️ 🥂 ♡

Classic Ladyfingers

3 egg whites, at room temperature

5 tablespoons + ¼ teaspoon sugar
for whipping egg whites

3 egg yolks at room temperature

3 tablespoons + 1 teaspoon sugar
for whipping egg yolks

½ cup + 2 tablespoons all purpose
flour, sifted

Confectioners' sugar for dusting

Tiramisu Cream

2 (8-ounce) packages mascarpone
cheese

3 eggs, separated

6 tablespoons sugar

3 tablespoons hazelnut liqueur

3 tablespoons dark rum

¼ cup coffee liqueur

1 cup heavy cream

Finishing

1¾ cups espresso or strong-brewed
coffee

⅓ cup cocoa powder

TIRAMISU IS AN ITALIAN VERSION of the English trifle (pages 25 to 27). Many people believe that it's a traditional Italian dessert that dates back generations, but in fact it was invented only in the 1980s in Treviso. Tiramisu is always served semifreddo ("semi-frozen" or "half-cold") and tastes best when the flavors are allowed to mingle. Ladyfingers can be made from scratch with this recipe or store-bought and layered with tiramisu cream. Either way, this dessert is easy to make in advance, so you can sit back and enjoy the party.

Prepare

1. Preheat oven to 350°F. Stack 4 baking sheets together in pairs: Doubling them up traps air and prevents ladyfingers from drying out. Line the top sheets with parchment paper.

Make

2. Fit a pastry bag with a #6 plain round pastry tip, and set it aside. Using a mixer with the whisk attachment, whip egg whites on medium-high speed until foamy. Add sugar on low speed. Whip on high speed until stiff peaks form.

3. In a clean bowl, whip egg yolks on medium-high speed for a few minutes. Slowly add sugar. Whip on high until pale and thick. Gently fold in whites and flour. Fill pastry bag with batter. Keeping the tip at a 45-degree angle to the pan, gently pipe 4-inch-long ladyfingers. Sift confectioners' sugar overtop. Bake 10 to 12 minutes or until golden. Let cool on sheets.

4. For the cream: In a saucepan over low heat, combine mascarpone, egg yolks, and sugar and cook until light in color. Let cool at least 20 minutes. Add hazelnut liqueur, rum, and 3 tablespoons coffee liqueur. In a mixing bowl, beat egg whites until stiff.

In another large bowl, whip cream until stiff peaks form. Fold egg whites, then whipped cream, into the mascarpone mixture.

Finish

5. Combine espresso with the remaining coffee liqueur. Place half a ladyfinger into the bottom of each cocktail glass. Soak with espresso–coffee liqueur and spoon a thin layer of tiramisu cream on top. Add layers of cookies and cream, ending with cream. Chill 2 hours. When ready to serve, top each glass with a ladyfinger and a sprinkle of cocoa powder.

Variation

Berry Tipsy Tiramisu
For the filling: In a saucepan, heat 1½ cups fresh berries with 1 cup sugar and ¼ cup water. Stir gently until sugar has dissolved and berries are well coated. Let cool. Layer ladyfingers with berry mixture and tiramisu cream.

Eggnog Tiramisu
For the filling: Prepare eggnog pastry cream (page 55) instead of tiramisu cream, but add 1½ cup mascarpone cheese and 3 tablespoons each of hazelnut and coffee liqueur.

Fast & Easy Tipsy Tiramisu
For the ladyfingers: Use store-bought ladyfingers.

Tropical Fruitcake Cupcakes

TYPE OF CAKE	SERVINGS	BAKING TIME	BOOZE METER	OCCASION
🧁	36	🕐 18 *to* 🕐 22	🙂	❄️ 🎀

Tropical Fruitcake Cupcakes
1½ cup assorted dried fruits, chopped
1 teaspoon fresh ginger, grated
½ cup golden raisins
¾ cup unsweetened flaked coconut
1 cup coconut rum
1¼ cup all-purpose flour
½ teaspoon baking powder
¼ teaspoon baking soda
½ teaspoon salt
1 teaspoon ground cardamom
½ cup (1 stick) unsalted butter
¾ cup dark brown sugar
1 egg
1 cup macadamia nuts or walnuts, chopped

Pineapple Rum Glaze
¼ cup sugar
¼ cup pineapple juice
Juice of one lemon
3 tablespoons light rum

Rum Ginger Cream-Cheese Frosting
1 (8-ounce) package cream cheese
6 tablespoons (¾ stick) unsalted butter
3 cups confectioners' sugar
1 tablespoon light rum
½ teaspoon ginger, freshly grated

Finishing
¼ cup unsweetened flaked coconut
¾ cup assorted dried pineapple, papaya, and mango
¼ cup candied ginger
¼ cup whole macadamia nuts or walnuts

OFTEN THE BUTT OF HOLIDAY JOKES, traditional fruitcake made with candied fruits, nuts, and spirits has been compared to a brick or a doorstop, thanks to the dense blockyness of its loafy form. But we are proud to say that we love fruitcake, and in order to thwart its bad rap, we've given it a makeover. Our little fruitcake cupcakes are nothing like the holiday dessert you've come to dread. They're cute, candylike, and chock-full of tropical flavors: pineapple, papaya, mango, ginger, and macadamia nuts. Complete the decadence by dousing with pineapple rum glaze and topping with rum ginger cream-cheese frosting. These little tropical treats will convert even the most skeptical scrooge into a fruitcake lover. They may even request the recipe.

Prepare

1. Preheat oven to 300°F. Grease and flour three 12-cup mini cupcake pans.

Make

2. In a bowl, combine dried fruits, ginger, raisins, coconut, and coconut rum. In another bowl, combine flour, baking powder, baking soda, salt, and cardamom; set aside.
3. In a mixing bowl, cream butter and sugar 3 to 5 minutes, or until light and fluffy. Beat in egg. Add flour mixture and fruit mixture to butter in three alternating additions, starting and finishing with flour. Stir in nuts.
4. Spoon batter into pans. Bake 18 to 22 minutes, or until a toothpick inserted in the center of a cupcake comes out clean. While cupcakes are in the oven, prepare the glaze.
5. For the glaze: In a saucepan over low heat, combine sugar, pineapple juice, and lemon juice; stir until sugar has dissolved. Remove from heat and stir in rum. While cupcakes are still hot, drizzle with

pineapple-rum glaze. Store remaining glaze in a container. Cover cupcakes and refrigerate overnight.

Finish

6. **For the frosting:** In a mixing bowl, beat cream cheese and butter until smooth and creamy. Sift in confectioners' sugar and beat to combine. Stir in rum and ginger.

7. Brush cupcakes with remaining pineapple rum glaze and then frost generously with rum ginger cream-cheese frosting. Sprinkle tops with coconut, dried fruit, candied ginger, and nuts.

Variations

Berry Fruitcake Cupcakes
For the mini cupcakes, glaze, and finishing. Replace pineapple, papaya, mango, and candied ginger with equal amounts dried raspberries, strawberries, cherries, and blueberries. Use pecans. Replace rum with berry liqueur.

Chocolate-Cherry Fruitcake Cupcakes
For the mini cupcakes, glaze, and finishing: Replace pineapple, papaya, and mango with 1 cup cherries and 1 cup chocolate chips. Replace rum with kirsch and use walnuts.

Layered Fruitcake Cupcakes
For mini layered cupcakes: Cut each mini cupcake in half and sandwich back together with a layer of rum ginger cream-cheese frosting. Top with more frosting, pineapple rum glaze, dried fruit, ginger, nuts, and coconut.

2 Cocktail Cakes

RECIPES BASED *on* COCKTAILS *and* MIXED DRINKS

In this chapter you'll find cakes, cupcakes, tea cakes, cheesecakes, and shortcakes inspired by cocktails: delightful concoctions made by mixing a distilled spirit with flavoring ingredients such as fruit juice, carbonated sodas, creams, or liqueurs. From the tropical Piña Colada Cake to the Top-Shelf Margarita Cheesecake to the party-perfect Rum-and-Coke Whoopie Pies, these confections are an indulgent cocktail-hour treat!

Amaretto Almond Delight Cake

TYPE OF CAKE	SERVINGS	BAKING TIME	BOOZE METER	OCCASION
🎂	⑧ to ⑩	⏰ 45	😄	🍽️ 🥂 ♡

Almond Delight Cake
¾ cup (1½ stick) unsalted butter
¾ cup sugar
1 (7-ounce) tube almond paste
Zest of 1 orange
Zest of 1 lemon
¼ cup amaretto liqueur
1 teaspoon vanilla extract
3 eggs
½ cup all-purpose flour
1 teaspoon baking powder

Amaretto Glaze
2 tablespoons apricot jam
¼ cup amaretto liqueur

Finishing
½ cup sliced almonds, toasted
½ cup confectioners' sugar

Variations

Chocolate Almond Delight Cake
For the topping: Drizzle with spiked chocolate sauce (page 59) instead of amaretto glaze and confectioners' sugar.

LOVE ALMONDS? Here's your cake. It's a light, sweet, slightly citrusy confection made with almond paste and amaretto. An almond liqueur from Italy, amaretto gets its name from *amaro*, the Italian word for "bitter" (as in bitter almond), or *amore*, the Italian word for "love." (So does that make *amaretto* a "bitter little love"?) Experiment with flavors by adding chocolate or reducing the amaretto and adding a splash of scotch or vodka. For a decorative touch, stencil patterns in confectioners' sugar on top of the cake; use fresh flowers or a paper doily for a lacy touch.

Prepare

1. Preheat oven to 350°F. Grease and flour a 9 inch springform cake pan.

Make

2. In a mixing bowl, cream butter and sugar 3 to 5 minutes, or until light and fluffy. Mix in almond paste, orange and lemon zests, amaretto, and vanilla. Beat in eggs, flour, and baking powder. Pour batter into the pan and bake 45 minutes, or until a knife inserted into the center comes out clean. Let cool.
3. For the glaze: In a saucepan over low heat, stir jam and amaretto together until smooth.

Finish

4. Unmold the cake onto a serving dish, and pour glaze overtop. Sprinkle with toasted almonds and a dusting of confectioners' sugar.

Eggnog Cream Cupcakes

TYPE OF CAKE	SERVINGS	BAKING TIME	BOOZE METER	OCCASION
🧁	⑫	⏰ *to* ⏰	☺	🍽 🥂 ❄

Eggnog Cupcakes
½ cup (1 stick) unsalted butter
1 cup sugar
2 eggs
¼ cup dark rum
½ cup milk
½ teaspoon vanilla extract
½ teaspoon almond extract
1¾ cups all-purpose flour
1 teaspoon baking powder
½ teaspoon salt
⅛ teaspoon allspice
¼ teaspoon ground cinnamon
⅛ teaspoon freshly grated nutmeg

Eggnog Pastry Cream
1 (3.3-ounce) box French vanilla instant
   pudding
1¾ cup milk
2 tablespoons light rum
¾ cup heavy cream

Rum-Spiked Whipped Cream
¼ cup brown sugar
¾ cup heavy cream
3 tablespoons rum

Finishing
¼ cup shaved chocolate

Variation
Chocolate Eggnog Cream Puffs
Skip the cake and use eggnog pastry
cream to fill chocolate cream puffs
(page 138).

WE LOVE THE HOLIDAYS because they are prime time for baking these comforting adults-only eggnog-infused cupcakes. No store-bought 'nog here—it's whipped into the pastry cream and topped off with rum. So put on some holiday music, relax, bake, and enjoy.

Prepare

1. Preheat oven to 350°F. Grease one 12-cup cupcake pan.

Make

2. In a mixing bowl, cream butter and sugar 3 to 5 minutes, or until light and fluffy. Beat in eggs. Mix in rum, milk, vanilla, and almond extract. In a separate bowl, combine flour, baking powder, salt, allspice, cinnamon, and nutmeg. Mix it into the batter until just combined. Fill cupcake pans two-thirds full and bake 20 to 22 minutes, or until a toothpick inserted in the center of a cupcake comes out clean.

3. For the eggnog pastry cream: Beat pudding powder and milk together on high speed 2 minutes or until the mixture begins to thicken. Stir in rum. In a separate bowl, beat cream until stiff peaks form, and then gently fold into the pudding mixture. Chill, covered, 1 hour.

4. For the whipped cream: In a bowl, beat brown sugar and about ¼ cup heavy cream at high speed, gradually adding the rest of the heavy cream until stiff peaks form. Gently fold in rum.

Finish

5. Once cupcakes are cooled, use a sharp knife to cut a hole two-thirds into each one, leaving a ⅛-inch rim around the top. Fill centers with eggnog pastry cream. Top each with a dollop of spiked whipped cream and garnish with shaved chocolate.

Harvey Wallbanger Cake

TYPE OF CAKE	SERVINGS	BAKING TIME	BOOZE METER	OCCASION
🍮	⑩	⏰ to ⏰	😄	🎁 👭

Boozy Golden Cake

1 box yellow cake mix

1 (3.3-ounce) box vanilla instant
  pudding

½ cup vegetable oil

4 eggs

¼ cup vodka

¼ cup Galliano liqueur

¾ cup orange juice

Orange Glaze

¼ cup orange juice

¼ cup confectioners' sugar

Boozy Orange Glaze

1 cup confectioners' sugar

1 tablespoon orange juice

1 tablespoon vodka

1 tablespoon Galliano liqueur

Finishing

¼ cup confectioners' sugar, optional

1 orange, sliced

ALL THE RAGE IN THE 1970S, the Harvey Wallbanger cocktail is a groovy twist on the classic Screwdriver: It adds a splash of the smooth vanilla Italian liqueur Galliano to the vodka and orange juice. In the seventies' spirit, this is one drunk Bundt cake that is dead easy to make! It's a light, moist, absolutely booze-drenched crowd-pleaser.

Prepare

1. Preheat oven to 350°F. Grease and flour a 10-inch Bundt pan.

Make

2. In a mixing bowl, beat cake mix, instant pudding powder, vegetable oil, eggs, vodka, Galliano, and orange juice for 4 minutes, or until smooth. Pour batter into the pan. Bake 45 to 50 minutes, or until golden brown.

Finish

3. For the glazes (choose one): In a bowl, combine all ingredients and mix until smooth and creamy. Drizzle over cake. Alternatively, you can garnish with orange slices or simply dust with confectioners' sugar.

Mint Julep Cupcakes

TYPE OF CAKE	SERVINGS	BAKING TIME	BOOZE METER	OCCASION
🧁	(12)	(15)	☺	🎁 🪑 🍸

Chocolate Mint Julep Cupcakes
½ cup (1 stick) unsalted butter
1 cup sugar
4 eggs
4 ounces bittersweet chocolate, melted and slightly cooled
1 cup all-purpose flour
1 teaspoon vanilla extract
3 teaspoons mint extract
1 tablespoon bourbon

Minty Whipped Cream
2 (8-ounce) packages cream cheese
½ cup confectioners' sugar
1 cup heavy cream
½ teaspoon mint extract

Spiked Chocolate Sauce
¼ cup heavy cream
½ cup sugar
2 ounces semisweet chocolate, chopped
1 tablespoon unsalted butter
1 tablespoon bourbon

Finishing
Sprigs of fresh mint

Variation

Grasshopper Cupcakes
For the cupcakes: Add ½ cup flaked coconut to the batter. For the cream: Reduce mint to 1 teaspoon and add 1 teaspoon coconut extract and 1 drop green food coloring.

TRADITIONALLY SERVED in a frosty silver cup, the Mint Julep is a mix of Kentucky bourbon, a little sugar, a little water, and a sprig of fresh mint. It's a refreshing bit of the Old South, and we've reinvented it as a light, chilled confection. These chocolate mint julep cupcakes are topped with a minty whipped cream and gooey, bourbon-spiked mint chocolate sauce.

Prepare

1. Preheat oven to 350°F. Grease and flour one 12-cup cupcake pan.

Make

2. In a mixing bowl, cream butter and sugar 3 to 5 minutes, or until light and fluffy. Beat in eggs one at a time. Mix in melted chocolate, flour, vanilla, and mint extract. Stir in bourbon. Spoon into the pan and bake 15 minutes, or until a toothpick inserted in the center of a cupcake comes out clean. Let cool completely.
3. For the whipped cream: Beat cream cheese and confectioners' sugar in a mixing bowl. Beat in heavy cream and mint extract. Refrigerate.
4. For the spiked chocolate sauce: In a saucepan over low heat, whisk together cream, sugar, chocolate, and butter until combined. Remove from heat and stir in bourbon. Let cool at least 15 minutes.

Finish

5. Split the cooled cupcakes in half and place bottom halves on individual serving plates. Top with cream. Replace the tops and spoon spiked chocolate sauce overtop. Garnish with sprigs of fresh mint.

Peachy Keen Fuzzy Navel Cupcakes

TYPE OF CAKE	SERVINGS	BAKING TIME	BOOZE METER	OCCASION
🧁	⑫	⏰ 20	☺	🪑 ⚥

Fuzzy Navel Cake
½ cup orange juice
½ cup peach schnapps
2½ cups all-purpose flour
1 tablespoon baking powder
½ teaspoon salt
½ cup (1 stick) unsalted butter
½ cup sugar
2 eggs
2 ripe peaches, diced

Fuzzy Navel Sauce
½ cup peach preserves
¼ cup orange marmalade
¼ cup orange juice
¼ cup peach schnapps

Roasted Peaches
6 ripe peaches, halved
2 tablespoons unsalted butter, melted
½ cup light brown sugar

OUR FUZZY NAVEL CUPCAKES are based on the highly popular cocktail invented during the Regan era—also known as the Michael Jackson, Madonna, and (the original) Rick Astley years. The drink's provocative name and sweet candy taste sped its rise in popularity among young clubbers. Its catchy name is actually quite innocent: "Fuzzy" refers to the Georgia peach, and "navel" refers to the Florida orange. However, the Fuzzy Navel's cocktail cousin Sex on the Beach (made with vodka and cranberry) is far from innocent—except when you see it on a family-restaurant menu as "Fun on the Beach."

Prepare

1. Preheat oven to 350°F. Grease and flour a 12-cup cupcake pan.

Make

2. For the cupcakes: Combine orange juice and peach schnapps and set aside. In a separate bowl, combine flour, baking powder, and salt.

3. In a mixing bowl, cream butter and sugar for 3 to 5 minutes, or until light and fluffy. Beat in the eggs one at a time. Add flour and juice mixtures to the batter in three alternating additions. When fully combined, beat for 1 minute. Gently stir in the peaches by hand. Spoon batter into the pan and bake for 20 minutes, or until a toothpick inserted comes out clean.

4. For the sauce: In a saucepan, combine peach preserves, marmalade, and orange juice, stirring occasionally. Once the mixture has thinned (about 5 minutes), remove from heat and stir in the peach schnapps.

5. For the roasted peaches: Line a baking sheet with aluminum foil

and put the peaches on top. Brush the tops with melted butter and sprinkle with brown sugar. Roast 25 to 35 minutes or until the sugar begins to bubble. Let cool, then remove and discard pits, and dice or slice peaches.

Finish

6. Place cupcakes on individual serving plates. Top with roasted peaches and drizzle with sauce.

Variations

Barbed Navel Cupcakes
For the cupcakes and sauce: Replace half of the peach schnapps with tequila, and half of the orange juice with lemonade.

Fuzzy Pucker Cupcakes
For the cupcakes and sauce: Substitute grapefruit juice for orange juice. Add grapefruit segments to the plate and cover with sauce.

Naked Navel Cupcakes
For the sauce and peaches: Use white peach schnapps and white peaches.

Sex-on-the-Beach Cupcakes
For the cupcakes and sauce: Replace half of the peach schnapps with vodka. Reduce the orange juice by two-thirds and add cranberry juice to volume. Stir ¾ cup cranberries into the batter. Stir in ½ cup cranberries and ¼ cup sugar to the sauce.

Woo Woo Cupcakes
For the cupcakes and sauce: Substitute cranberry juice for orange juice.

The 1980s make us think of Studio 54, disco, and cocaine—not cocktails. However, '80s cocktails are lots of fun: the Fuzzy Navel, the Sloe Comfortable Screw, Midori Melon Balls, Sex on the Beach, the Woo Woo, and Long Island Iced Teas, to mention a few. Despite their names and appearances, these colorful candy-flavored cocktails are potent drinks that sneak up on you and can deliver major hangovers. They ruled the 1980s club scene until Mothers Against Drunk Driving (MADD) became a big influence in the late '80s, raising consciousness about the toll of intoxication and putting a damper on the whole "party hardy and drive" thing.

As a result, there was a wine-bar boom in the early 1990s, and white wines like Chablis became much more popular than cocktails, at least among the ladies. This trend led to the development of all sorts of wine coolers and alco-pops like Zima. Because everything old is new again, there was another renaissance of cocktail culture in the late '90s: Time-honored drinks such as Martinis and Gimlets came back into style, and the bartenders' art was once again appreciated. But that doesn't mean we can't enjoy a few outrageous '80s cocktails every once in a while. For a boozy brunch, pair these cocktails with cupcakes and cancel all afternoon engagements.

Fuzzy Navel
2 ounces peach schnapps
6 ounces fresh orange juice
Fruit of choice

Pour the schnapps and orange juice over ice in a chilled glass. Garnish with fruit if desired.

Woo Woo Substitute cranberry juice for the orange juice.

Sex on the Beach
2 ounces vodka
2 ounces peach schnapps
3 ounces fresh orange juice or grapefruit juice
2 ounces cranberry juice

Stir to combine all ingredients over ice in a glass. Garnish with fruit or a ridiculously big tropical cocktail garnish.

After Sex Combine 2 ounces vodka and 1 ounce crème de banana.

Orgasm Combine 1 ounce amaretto, 1 ounce Kahlúa, and 1 ounce coffee liqueur, such as Bailey's Irish Cream.

Piña Colada Cake

Piña Colada Cake
½ cup (1 stick) unsalted butter
1¾ cups sugar
¾ cup coconut rum
½ cup sweetened cream of coconut
4 eggs
2¾ cups all-purpose flour
1 teaspoon baking powder
½ teaspoon baking soda
½ teaspoon salt
½ cup milk
½ cup sour cream

Coconut Cream Cheese Frosting
2 (8-ounce) packages cream cheese
½ cup (1 stick) unsalted butter
¼ cup sweetened cream of coconut
½ teaspoon vanilla extract
¼ cup coconut rum
1 cup confectioners' sugar

Finishing
½ cup crushed pineapple, drained well
1 (10-ounce) package sweetened flaked coconut, toasted
A few maraschino cherries, optional

Variation
Snow White Piña Colada Cake
For the finishing: Leave the coconut untoasted.

THE PIÑA COLADA IS THE OFFICIAL COCKTAIL of Puerto Rico. It also served as the inspiration for Rupert Holmes's 1979 hit song "Escape," which everyone knows as "The Piña Colada Song" because of its lyrics about disenchanted love and enjoyment of a certain little coconut cocktail. A Piña Colada is an icy, creamy, fruity rum drink that means summer sun and fun. This cake does, too!

Prepare

1. Preheat oven to 350°F. Grease and flour two 9-inch cake pans.

Make

2. In a mixing bowl, beat butter, sugar, coconut rum, and cream of coconut 3 to 5 minutes, or until smooth. Beat in eggs one at a time. In a separate bowl, combine flour, baking powder, baking soda, and salt. In another bowl, whisk together milk and sour cream. Mix in the flour and milk mixtures in three alternating additions.
3. Pour batter into pans and bake 30 minutes, or until a knife inserted in the center comes out clean. Let cool.
4. For the frosting: In a mixing bowl, beat together cream cheese, butter, cream of coconut, vanilla, and coconut rum until light and fluffy. Beat in confectioners' sugar. Refrigerate until cakes are cooled.

Finish

5. Place one cake layer on a serving plate and top with frosting. Add a layer of crushed pineapple and half the toasted coconut. Place second layer on top. Spread the rest of the frosting over the cake and sprinkle with the remaining coconut.

Pumpkin Martini Cakes

TYPE OF CAKE	SERVINGS	BAKING TIME	BOOZE METER	OCCASION
🧁 or 🍰🍰	⑫	⏰ to ⏰	☺	❄

Pumpkin Martini Cakes
½ cup (1 stick) unsalted butter
1⅓ cups dark brown sugar
2 eggs
2 cups all-purpose flour
2 teaspoons baking powder
¼ teaspoon baking soda
2½ teaspoons pumpkin pie spice
½ teaspoon salt
½ cup milk
1¼ cups pumpkin puree, canned or fresh
1 teaspoon vanilla extract
¼ cup bourbon or vodka
2 tablespoons triple sec

Pumpkin Spiked Maple Glaze
½ cup Grade-A maple syrup
3 tablespoons unsalted butter
3 tablespoons pumpkin butter
⅛ teaspoon salt
½ cup bourbon or vodka
2 tablespoons triple sec

Finishing
1 cup roasted pumpkin seeds

Spiked Cream-Cheese Frosting
1 (8-ounce) package cream cheese
6 tablespoons (¾ stick) unsalted butter
3 cups confectioners' sugar
1 tablespoon bourbon or vodka

NATIVE AMERICANS USED PUMPKINS for medicinal purposes, and the fruit has long been valued for its curative properties. At one time, pumpkins were even recommended for removing freckles and curing snakebites. We have brought those restorative qualities to our pumpkin martini cakes, based on the Pumpkin Martini, a popular holiday drink. Relaxing by a fire on a brisk autumn day eating our spicy cake soaked in a vodka- or bourbon-spiked pumpkin maple glaze will definitely soothe your soul.

Prepare

1. Preheat the oven to 350°F. Grease individual-size cake pans or a mini cupcake pan.

Make

2. In a mixing bowl, cream butter and sugar 3 to 5 minutes, or until light and fluffy. Add eggs one at a time, beating after each addition.
3. In a separate bowl combine the flour, baking powder, baking soda, pumpkin pie spice, and salt. Add to the butter mixture with the milk in three alternating additions. Mix in pumpkin, vanilla, bourbon (or vodka), and triple sec and beat until smooth.
4. Fill pans three-quarters full. Bake 20 to 25 minutes, or until a toothpick inserted in the center comes out clean. Let cool.
5. For the glaze: In a saucepan, bring the maple syrup, butter, pumpkin butter, and salt to a boil. Lower to a simmer for 2 to 3 minutes. Stir in bourbon (or vodka) and triple sec and heat for 1 minute more.

Pumpkin Apple Raisin Martini Cakes
For the cakes: Increase bourbon to
⅓ cup. Replace triple sec with anise
liqueur. Stir in 1 cup cubed fresh apple
and ¾ cup raisins. For the glaze: Add
3 tablespoons apple butter.

Pumpkin Chip Martini Cakes
For the cakes: Add 1½ cup chocolate
chips to the batter.

Finish

6. Fill martini glasses with cakes and pumpkin seeds. Drizzle with
   boozy pumpkin maple glaze.
7. For the frosting: In a mixing bowl, beat cream cheese and butter
   until combined. Beat in confectioners' sugar. Stir in the bourbon
   (or vodka) and top the martini cakes with frosting.

PUMPKIN MARTINI

Believe it or not, the martini is one of the oldest cocktails: It dates
back to about 1862, when it was called the Martinez. Legend has it
that a San Francisco bartender created this potent concoction for
a miner on his way to the Gold Rush in the town of Martinez. We
don't think of martinis as a gold miners' drink. To most of us, it's
a swanky 1960s cocktail that was both James Bond's and the mad
Madison Avenue advertising executives' drink of choice.

The Pumpkin Martini is a more recent invention, a descendant
of the Vodkatini and other nontraditional flavor variations made
without gin. If you happen to come across pumpkin vodka, pumpkin
schnapps, or pumpkin liqueur, snatch it up because it can be diffi-
cult to find. Otherwise, try using a bit of strained pumpkin puree
(fresh or canned) to flavor simple syrup (page 133) or vodka (page
131). Cream liqueurs and coffee cream liqueurs also work well in
a Pumpkin Martini. Other liquors commonly mixed with pumpkin
flavors include bourbon, whiskey, and spiced rum. Experiment and
adjust measurements to taste.

Pumpkin Martini
2 ounces vanilla vodka
1 ounce cream or cream liqueur
½ ounce pumpkin liqueur or
  pumpkin-infused simple syrup

Shake liqueurs with ice
and strain into a chilled
martini glass. Garnish with
a cinnamon stick, roasted
pumpkin seeds, or nutmeg.

Punch Drunk Marble Cake

TYPE OF CAKE	SERVINGS	BAKING TIME	BOOZE METER	OCCASION
🍲	(16)	⏰(30)	☺	🎁 ⚢

Punch Drunk Marble Cake
1 (16-ounce) can fruit cocktail,
   in light syrup
¾ cup light rum, divided
1 cup (2 sticks) unsalted butter
2 cups sugar
4 eggs
½ cup orange juice
¼ cup lime juice
½ cup milk
4 cups all-purpose flour
2 tablespoons baking powder
¾ teaspoon salt
Several drops of three different shades
   of food coloring

Spiked Whipped Cream
3 cups (1 pint) heavy cream
5 tablespoons sugar
2 tablespoons Curaçao (or other liqueur)

Finishing
½ cup sprinkles

Variations

Holiday Punch Drunk Cake
For the cake: Limit the food coloring
to red and green. For the finishing: Add
nuts. Replace cherries with cooked
cranberries.

Sherbet Punch Drunk Cake
For the filling: Replace or supplement
spiked whipped cream with 1 gallon
rainbow sherbet.

WHOLESOME CHURCH SOCIALS and school functions wouldn't be the same without big bowls of candy-colored fruit punch. If you've ever wanted to slip in some alcohol to loosen up the crowd, this is your cake! It's a brightly colored, over-the-top party treat layered in a large punch bowl with spiked whipped cream, coconut, and sprinkles, or whatever toppings you like. Scoop it into punch cups to serve.

Prepare

1. Preheat oven to 350°F. Grease and flour three 9-inch round cake pans. Set aside a punch bowl that is bigger than the cake pans.

Make

2. Soak fruit cocktail in ½ cup rum. Cover and refrigerate.
3. In a mixing bowl, cream butter and sugar 3 to 5 minutes, or until light and fluffy. Beat in eggs. Mix in orange and lime juices, milk, and ¼ cup rum. Mix in flour, baking powder, and salt. Pour batter into pans. Add a few drops of food coloring to each pan; swirl coloring through batter to create a marbleized look. Bake 25 to 30 minutes, or until a knife inserted in the center comes out clean.
4. For the whipped cream: In a mixing bowl, beat cream and sugar until stiff peaks form. Gently fold in Curaçao.

Finish

5. Place one layer of cake in the punch bowl. Layer cream and rum-soaked fruit on top. Repeat with the next two layers. Top with sprinkles. Serve in individual punch cups with big spoons.

Rum & Coke Whoopie Pies

TYPE OF CAKE	SERVINGS	BAKING TIME	BOOZE METER	OCCASION
🧁🍰	(8)	⏰(10)	☺	🪑 ⚲

Chocolate Soda Cakes
½ cup (1 stick) unsalted butter
1 cup sugar
2 eggs
1 teaspoons vanilla extract
½ cup buttermilk
¼ cup cola
2½ cups all-purpose flour
5 tablespoons unsweetened cocoa
  powder
1 teaspoon baking soda
1 teaspoon baking powder
½ teaspoon salt

Fluffy Rum-Spiked Cream Filling
½ cup (1 stick) unsalted butter
1 cup marshmallow fluff
3 or 4 tablespoons rum
2 cups confectioners' sugar

Finishing
Confectioners' sugar for dusting,
  if desired
Mini chocolate chips for rolling,
  if desired

Variation
Kid-Friendly Whoopie Pies
Replace rum in the filling with cola or
root beer.

BOTH THE PENNSYLVANIA DUTCH and New Englanders claim to have dreamed up whoopie pies. We don't know who invented them, but we do know that sweet creamy frosting sandwiched between mini chocolate cakes is divine! The filling can be made with store-bought marshmallow fluff or homemade Fluffy Marshmallow Crème (page 139) and spiked with rum. Pair this delight with a classic Rum & Coke cocktail for the ultimate in tipsy indulgence.

Prepare

1. Preheat oven to 375°F. Line two baking sheets with parchment paper or silicone baking mats.

Make

2. In a mixing bowl, cream butter and sugar 3 to 5 minutes, or until light and fluffy. Beat in eggs and vanilla. In another bowl, combine buttermilk and cola. Add it to creamed butter and egg mixture. Beat in flour, cocoa, baking soda, baking powder, and salt.
3. Drop batter by the tablespoonful onto baking sheets, leaving plenty of room for the cakes to spread; bake 10 minutes. Let cool completely.
4. For the cream filling: In a mixing bowl, beat together butter and marshmallow fluff until light and creamy. Mix in rum. Slowly beat in confectioners' sugar, mixing until light and fluffy.

Finish

5. Sandwich a generous amount of filling between the cooled cakes. To glamorize, dust tops with confectioners' sugar or roll the fluffy cream edges in mini chocolate chips or sprinkles.

Strawberry Daiquiri Shortcakes

TYPE OF CAKE	SERVINGS	BAKING TIME	BOOZE METER	OCCASION
🥧	⑧	⏰15 to ⏰18	☺	☼ 🎋 🎁

Strawberry Shortcakes
½ cup (1 stick) unsalted butter
½ cup sugar
2 eggs
½ teaspoon vanilla extract
¼ cup rum
1 cup all-purpose flour
½ teaspoon salt
¼ cup strawberry yogurt
1 cup strawberries, chopped

Strawberry Mascarpone Fluff
1 (8 ounce) package mascarpone cheese
⅔ cup confectioners' sugar
1 teaspoon rum
1 teaspoon strawberry jam
1 cup heavy cream

Garnish
8 fresh sliced strawberries or candied
   strawberries (page 137)

Variation

Banana Daiquiri Shortcakes
For the shortcakes: Use lemon-lime rum
or crème de banana, replace strawberry
yogurt with banana yogurt, and replace
fresh strawberries with sliced banana.
For the fluff: Replace regular rum with
lemon-lime rum, omit jam, and replace
strawberry with 2 tablespoons mashed
banana.

FROZEN OR STRAIGHT UP, the Daiquiri's combination of fruit, sugar, and rum is completely refreshing. It's one of those delicious cocktails that sneak up on you because the tangy sweet flavor masks the taste of alcohol. Daiquiris became popular in the 1940s, when they were made famous by the El Floridita bar in Havana, one of Ernest Hemmingway's favorite haunts. These tipsy little shortcakes are filled with strawberry mascarpone fluff and garnished with fresh sliced strawberries or jewel-like candied strawberries.

Prepare

1. Preheat oven to 350°F. Grease and flour 8 cups in a 12-cup muffin pan.

Make

2. In a mixing bowl, beat butter and sugar 3 to 5 minutes, or until light and fluffy. Beat in eggs one at a time. Mix in vanilla and rum; then add flour and salt. Fold in yogurt and strawberries. Pour batter into prepared muffin cups and bake 15 to 18 minutes, or until golden brown around the edges.
3. For the fluff: In a mixing bowl, beat together cheese, sugar, rum, jam, and cream until smooth and fluffy.

Finish

4. Place cooled cakes on individual serving dishes or crumble them into cups. Top each with fluff and fresh sliced strawberries.

Tequila Sunrise Cake

TYPE OF CAKE	SERVINGS	BAKING TIME	BOOZE METER	OCCASION
🍮	⑩	⏰ to ⏰ (40 to 45)	☺	☀

Tequila Sunrise Cake

¾ cup (1½ stick) unsalted butter

1 cup sugar

Zest of 1 orange

3 eggs

¾ cup sour cream

2¼ cups all-purpose flour

½ teaspoon salt

2 teaspoons baking powder

½ teaspoon baking soda

⅓ cup fresh orange juice

2 tablespoons Curaçao

2 tablespoons tequila

¼ cup pomegranate juice

A few drops red food coloring

Curaçao Glaze

½ cup sugar

⅓ cup orange juice

2 tablespoons Curaçao

¼ cup confectioners' sugar

Finishing

⅓ cup pomegranate seeds, optional

THIS COLORFUL CAKE IS INSPIRED BY the popular cocktail made from tequila, orange juice, and grenadine. The name *grenadine* comes from the French word *grenade*, meaning "pomegranate," although modern-day grenadine is made from corn syrup and artificial flavorings. We've brought the pomegranate back for a sunny dessert that's sure to brighten your day. To get the cocktail's signature look, gently scoop color-tinted batter into the pan so it sinks into the cake like a beautiful Tequila Sunrise.

Prepare

1. Preheat oven to 350°F. Grease and flour a 9-inch Bundt pan.

Make

2. In a mixing bowl, cream butter, sugar, and zest 3 to 5 minutes, or until light and fluffy. Beat in eggs one at a time. Mix in sour cream.

3. In a separate bowl, combine flour, salt, baking powder, and baking soda. Add flour mixture and orange juice to butter mixture in three alternating additions. Stir in Curaçao and tequila. Pour two-thirds of batter into the pan. Add pomegranate juice and food color to the remaining batter and gently spread it over the center of the first layer. Bake 40 to 45 minutes, or until a knife inserted in the center comes out clean.

Finish

4. For the glaze: In a saucepan over low heat, stir sugar and orange juice 2 minutes, or until sugar has dissolved. Remove from heat and stir in Curaçao and confectioners' sugar. Spoon glaze over the cooled cake. Sprinkle with pomegranate seeds and serve.

Variations

Caribbean Sunrise Layer Cake

Bake the pomegranate batter and the orange batter in 9-inch round cake pans for 25 to 30 minutes. Soak the layers in Pineapple Rum Glaze (page 47), and fill and top the cake with Coconut Cream Cheese Frosting (page 65).

Tequila Sunset Cake

Replace pomegranate juice with blackberry juice and blackberry; replace pomegranate liquor with brandy.

THE ORIGINAL TEQUILA SUNRISE

The Tequila Sunrise cocktail was invented in the late 1930s or early 1940s by bartender Gene Sulit at the Arizona Biltmore, then a fashionable playground for the rich and famous. The original ingredients—tequila, crème de cassis, lime juice, and soda water—separate when poured, mimicking a sunrise. To this day, the beverage is the perfect companion while sitting poolside.

Tequila Sunrise
1½ ounces white tequila, iced
4 ounces cold, fresh orange juice
Dash of grenadine
Slice of orange

Pour the tequila into a chilled highball glass, followed by the orange juice. Float the grenadine on top, and garnish with an orange slice.

Tequila Sunset Replace grenadine with blackberry brandy, and garnish with a marachino cherry.

Malibu Sunrise Substitute Malibu coconut rum for the tequila.

Top-Shelf Margarita Cheesecake

TYPE OF CAKE	SERVINGS	BAKING TIME	BOOZE METER	OCCASION
⬭	⑩	⏰ 60	☺	🍽 🥂

Cornmeal Crust

½ cup (1 stick) unsalted butter

¼ cup sugar

½ cup all-purpose flour

½ cup yellow cornmeal

¼ teaspoon coarse salt

Margarita Cheesecake

3 (8 ounce) packages cream cheese

1 cup sugar

4 eggs

¼ cup fresh lime juice

2 tablespoons tequila

2 tablespoons triple sec

Zest of half a lime

Margarita Whipped Cream

1 cup heavy cream

½ cup confectioners' sugar

1 tablespoon fresh lime juice

2 tablespoons high-quality tequila

2 tablespoons triple sec

Garnish

3 limes, sliced soaked in 1 cup simple syrup (page 133)

Coarse salt, to taste

IF YOU ASK A BARTENDER for a "top-shelf Margarita," he will give you a nod of respect and grab a bottle of excellent-quality tequila for a special cocktail made with triple sec and fresh lemon or lime juice. For our top-shelf cheesecake, we've replaced the traditional crushed pretzel or graham cracker crust with a savory cornmeal one worthy of this sweet, creamy, five-star dessert.

Prepare

1. Preheat oven to 350°F. Grease bottom and sides of a 9 inch spring-form pan.

Make

2. In a mixing bowl, cream butter and sugar 3 to 5 minutes, or until light and fluffy. Gradually add flour, cornmeal, and salt and mix to combine. Press the mixture into the bottom of the pan and bake 15 to 20 minutes, or until golden brown. Let cool.

3. For the cheesecake: In a mixing bowl, combine cream cheese and sugar and beat 4 to 5 minutes, or until smooth. Beat in eggs one at a time. Stir in lime juice, tequila, tripe sec, and lime zest.

4. Spread mixture into the cooled crust and bake 45 to 50 minutes. Remove from oven and let cool 1 hour. Transfer to refrigerator and chill at least 6 hours or overnight.

5. For the whipped cream: In a mixing bowl, combine cream, confectioners' sugar, lime juice, tequila, and triple sec; starting on low speed and gradually increasing to high, beat until soft peaks form.

TOP-SHELF MARGARITA CHEESECAKE

Melon Margarita Cheesecake
For the cheesecake: Replace triple sec with melon liqueur. Top with fresh sliced melon.

Peach Margarita Cheesecake
For the cheesecake and cream: Replace triple sec with peach schnapps. After crust has cooled, spread 1¼ cup thinly sliced peaches on the bottom; spoon cheesecake mixture overtop. When ready to serve, top with fresh peaches.

Strawberry Margarita Cheesecake
For the topping and cream: After crust has cooled, spread 1¼ cup thinly sliced strawberries on the bottom; spoon cheesecake mixture overtop. When ready to serve, top with fresh strawberries.

Finish

6. Let the cheesecake sit at room temperature for 30 minutes. Spread the Margarita cream on top. Drain the lime slices from the simple syrup. Sprinkle a pinch of coarse salt around the edge of the crust and top the cheesecake with limes.

CLASSIC COCKTAILS FROM THE 1940s

The 1940s saw the war and rationing, but cocktails like the Manhattan, Tom Collins, Whiskey Sour, and Gin Rickey were popular. Apparently there was also a surplus of Smirnoff vodka at that time, so the Moscow Mule was created. The Margarita was popularized in the late '40s. Then with all the returning soldiers and the growth of the suburbs, cocktails at home became the thing to do in 1950s America. There was an emerging interest in ethnic foods and themed dinner parties. This meant enjoying both old familiar and new cocktails ideas, such as Vodka Gimlets, Singapore Slings, and Sea Breezes. Decades later the simple, refreshing Margarita is still a classic.

Margarita
Wedge of lime and coarse sea salt for rimming
2 ounces tequila
¾ ounce fresh lime juice
1 ounce Cointreau or triple sec
Wedge of lime to garnish

Rim a margarita glass with lime and salt, and chill briefly. Shake the tequila, lime juice, and Cointreau with ice; strain into the chilled glass. Add ice if desired. Garnish with another lime wedge.

Blue Margarita Add ¾ ounce blue Curaçao.

Frozen Margarita In a blender, combine the ingredients along with 2 teaspoons superfine sugar or simple syrup (page 133), ½ cup chopped fresh strawberries, and about 1 cup of cracked ice. Process until frothy.

3 Cake Shots

RECIPES *for the* ULTIMATE PARTY SNACK

Any Booze Cake can be turned into a cake shot by cutting it into bite-size pieces or using mini cupcake pans for the batter. This chapter is full of sophisticated single-serving treats, from Rum Mocha Brownie Bites to fragrant Wine-Tasting Cakes in merlot, chardonnay, or rosé, not to mention party-perfect snacks, from Jelly Cake Shots to Long Island Iced Tea Cakes. Party!

Blue Hawaii Pineapple Upside-Down Cupcakes

TYPE OF CAKE	SERVINGS	BAKING TIME	BOOZE METER	OCCASION
🧁	⑩ to ⑫	⏰25 to ⏰30	☺	🏕 ⚥

Spiked Pineapple Cupcakes
6 tablespoons (¾ stick) unsalted butter
1 cup sugar
2 eggs
1 teaspoon vanilla extract
2½ tablespoons rum
¼ cup pineapple juice
¼ cup sweet-and-sour mix (store-bought or homemade, page 133)
1¼ cups all-purpose flour
1½ teaspoons baking powder
¼ teaspoon salt
1½ tablespoons blue Curaçao
A few drops blue food coloring

Rum Pineapple Topping
½ cup (1 stick) unsalted butter
⅓ cup brown sugar
2 or 3 tablespoons rum
10 pineapple rings

Finishing
spiked whipped cream (page 142)
½ cup sweetened flaked coconut (toasted or untoasted)
10 maraschino cherries

SWEET-AND-SOUR PINEAPPLE CUPCAKES combine the tropical flavors of a Blue Hawaii Cocktail—blue Curaçao, pineapple, and rum—with the classic pineapple upside-down cake. Don't have too many, or things might get a little upside down for you, too!

Prepare

1. Preheat oven to 350°F. Grease 10 ramekins or one cupcake pan. (Pineapple rings can fit into most ramekins, large cupcake cups, or mini cake molds; or cut pineapple into wedges to fit your pan.)

Make

2. In a mixing bowl, cream butter and sugar until light and fluffy. Mix in eggs. Stir in vanilla, rum, pineapple juice, and sweet-and-sour mix. Add flour, baking powder, and salt. Transfer one-third of the batter into a separate bowl and stir in blue Curaçao and food coloring.

3. For the topping: In a saucepan over medium heat, stir butter and brown sugar 3 minutes, or until melted. Remove from heat and stir in rum. Drop a spoonful of sauce and a pineapple ring into each ramekin or cupcake cup. Spoon yellow batter into pans. Refrigerate 30 minutes (chilling keeps the colored layers separate). Add blue batter, filling each cup almost to the top. Bake 25 to 30 minutes.

Finish

5. Loosen cooled cakes with a knife. Press a tray to the cupcake pan or ramekins; flip over to unmold. Top each with spiked whipped cream, coconut, and a maraschino cherry.

Jelly Cake Shots

TYPE OF CAKE	SERVINGS	BAKING TIME	BOOZE METER	OCCASION
🔌	12 to 18	25 to 30	😃	👯

Boozy Cake

½ cup (1 stick) unsalted butter

2 cups sugar

4 eggs, separated

1 cup whole milk

1 teaspoon vanilla extract

3 tablespoons liquor

3 cups all purpose flour

4 teaspoons baking powder

½ teaspoon salt

Jelly Shots

1½ cups powdered gelatin

2¼ cups water or juice

½ cup liquor

Finish

Fruit, chocolate chips, flavored liqueurs, candies, or cocktail picks

Variation

Super-Easy Boozy Cake

For the cake: Make boozy cake in minutes by substituting your liquor of choice in the recipe on page 57 and layering with a batch of Jelly Shots.

FORGET JELL-O SHOTS. Jelly Cake Shots are the ultimate party treat! Bake them in silicone molds for fun shapes, such as hearts, flowers, or stars, and layer colors. Mix-in ingredients, such as fruit chunks, chocolate chips, or candies, only add to the fun! The recipe is easy to adapt to your favorite liquor or cocktail (page 86).

Prepare

1. Preheat oven to 350°F. Grease a 9-by-13-inch sheet cake pan or individually portioned silicone baking molds.

Make

2. In a mixing bowl, cream butter and sugar 3 to 5 minutes, or until light and fluffy. Beat in egg yolks and milk; stir in vanilla and liquor. Mix in flour, baking powder, and salt.
3. In a separate bowl, beat egg whites until stiff. Gently fold egg whites into the batter. Fill the pan or molds two-thirds full and bake 25 to 30 minutes.
4. For the Jelly Shot: In a saucepan, bring 2¼ cups water or juice to a boil; stir in gelatin until dissolved. Remove from heat and let cool about 20 minutes. Stir in alcohol. Refrigerate until gelatin just begins to set; drop in fruit or other mix-ins, if desired.
5. Pour into a 9-by-13-inch pan (or dish) and refrigerate at least 3 hours. Prepare and chill a second jelly shot in a separate pan, if desired.

Finish

6. Slice cake into shapes or unmold. Slice jelly shots to match and stack the layers in shot glasses or on trays. Garnish with toppings or cocktail picks. Party!

30 to 50 proof alcohol: 1½ cups water or juice
80 to 100 proof alcohol: 1¼ cups water or juice
150 to 200 proof alcohol: ¾ cup water or juice

FLAVORED SHOTS GUIDE

Use these combinations in the Jelly Shot recipe, or mix your own. Flavored gelatin can always be replaced with unflavored gelatin and a few tablespoons of simple syrup (page 133).

Appletini Cake Shots: Apple gelatin, apple juice, vodka, apple schnapps, and triple sec

Blue Hawaii Cake Shots: Blueberry gelatin, pineapple juice, blue Curaçao

Cherry Cake Shots: Cherry gelatin, water, cherry liqueur or cherry brandy, and maraschino cherries

Chocolate Cake Shots: Unflavored gelatin with simple syrup; ¼ cup chocolate syrup, chocolate pieces, mini marshmallows, and chocolate liqueur

Coffee Cake Shots: Unflavored gelatin, cooled coffee, and coffee liqueur

Cosmo Cake Shots: Raspberry gelatin, cranberry juice, vodka, lime, and triple sec

Kamikaze Cake Shots: Lime gelatin, vodka, and triple sec

Licorice Cake Shots: Unflavored gelatin with simple syrup, 1 teaspoon licorice extract, anisette liqueur, and licorice candies

Margarita Cake Shots: Lime gelatin, margarita mix, lemonade, tequila, and lime slices

Mojito Cake Shots: Lime gelatin, water, light rum, and fresh mint leaves

Piña Colada Cake Shots: Piña Colada gelatin and pineapple juice, coconut-flavored rum, and sweetened flaked coconut

Pineapple Cake Shots: Pineapple gelatin, water, light rum, and pineapple chunks

Rum & Coke Cake Shots: Unflavored or wild cherry gelatin, cola, and rum

Screwdriver Cake Shots: Orange gelatin, water, orange-flavored vodka, and mandarin oranges

Strawberry Daiquiri Cake Shots: Strawberry gelatin, water, light rum, and sliced strawberries

Tequila Sunrise Cake Shots: Orange gelatin, water, tequila, triple sec, and grenadine

Watermelon Cake Shots: Watermelon gelatin, water, and watermelon-flavored vodka or watermelon-flavored schnapps

Wine Cake Shots: Unflavored or grape gelatin with wine and grapes

ALTERNATE SERVING SUGGESTION

For super-easy jelly cake shots that don't even need to be assembled, try this method based on the classic American Jell-O cake or "poke cake" (so-called because fork holes poked into spongy cake allow Jell-O to soak into the cake in colorful drips).

For the Jelly Shot (page 85): In a saucepan, bring 2¼ cups water or juice to a boil; stir in gelatin until dissolved. Remove from heat and let cool about 20 minutes. Stir in alcohol. Refrigerate until gelatin just begins to set; drop in fruit or other mix-ins, if desired. Spread gelatin evenly over cooled cake and refrigerate at least 3 hours. Prepare a second Jelly Shot (if desired) and pour over the set first layer. Refrigerate overnight.

Long Island Iced Tea Cakes

TYPE OF CAKE	SERVINGS	BAKING TIME	BOOZE METER	OCCASION
🍢	20 to 28	20 to 22	😃	🎁 ⚢

Long Island Iced Tea Cakes
2 cups cake flour
½ teaspoon baking soda
½ teaspoon baking powder
¼ teaspoon salt
1 teaspoon vanilla extract
1 tablespoon gin
1 tablespoon light rum
1 tablespoon tequila
1 tablespoon vodka
1 tablespoon triple sec
2 tablespoons fresh lemon juice
2 tablespoons cola, chilled
1 cup sugar, divided
½ cup milk
6 egg yolks
½ cup (1 stick) unsalted butter

Long Island Iced Tea Soaking Sauce
1 tablespoon gin
1 tablespoon light rum
1 tablespoon tequila
1 tablespoon vodka
1 tablespoon triple sec
2 tablespoons fresh lemon juice
1 teaspoon sugar
2 tablespoons cold cola

Variations

Frosted Long Island Ice Tea Cakes
For frosting: Spike marshmallow crème (page 139) with same amount of all booze ingredients as cakes. Frost and sprinkle with lemon zest.

MANY A WILD AND CRAZY NIGHT has started out innocently enough with a Long Island Iced Tea—a potent concoction of a lot of white alcohols (vodka, rum, gin, and tequila). Nicely spiked with one of these intoxicating cocktails, this golden pound cake is baked and then soaked in *another* cocktail. Cut into bite-size pieces and skewered with cocktail picks, these libation-like nibbles make party-perfect finger food.

Prepare

1. Preheat oven to 350°F. Grease and flour a 9-by-13-inch cake pan.

Make

2. In a bowl, combine flour, baking soda, baking powder, and salt; set aside. In a glass measuring cup, combine vanilla, gin, rum, tequila, vodka, triple sec, lemon juice, cola, 1 teaspoon of the sugar, and milk. (Don't worry if the alcohol curdles the milk.)
3. In a mixing bowl, beat the egg yolks 5 minutes, or until thick and pale. Add ½ cup sugar and beat until yolks form a thick ribbon. Gradually beat in the butter and remaining sugar.
4. Beat in flour and milk mixtures in three alternating additions. Pour batter into the pan. Bake 20 to 22 minutes, or until a knife inserted in the center comes out clean. Let cool completely.

Finish

5. For the soaking sauce: While the cake cools, combine all ingredients in the cleaned and dried cake pan. Cut cake into bite-size pieces; return them to the pan to soak up the sauce, about 30 minutes to 1 hour. To serve, arrange tea cakes on a platter with cocktail picks.

Mexican Chocolate Cakes with Tequila Cajeta Caramel Sauce

TYPE OF CAKE	SERVINGS	BAKING TIME	BOOZE METER	OCCASION
	12	15	😃	♀♀

Flourless Chocolate Cakes

½ cup (1 stick) unsalted butter

½ cup sugar, divided

9 ounces semisweet dark chocolate, chopped

1 teaspoon vanilla extract

2 eggs, separated

1 tablespoon coffee liqueur (store-bought or homemade, page 130)

½ teaspoon salt

Tequila Cajeta Caramel Sauce

½ cup tequila

½ cup cajeta or caramel sauce

FLOURLESS CHOCOLATE CAKES are usually heavy and dense. Not this one. We've lightened the texture, and a dash of coffee liqueur gives it an extra-rich flavor. The sauce is made of tequila melted into *cajeta*—a devilishly good Mexican caramel. You can use store-bought cajeta or regular caramel sauce. Either way, it's a rich, gooey, sticky delight. *Fiesta!*

Prepare

1. Preheat oven to 425°F. Grease and flour a 12-cup cupcake pan.

Make

2. In a saucepan over medium-low heat, melt butter with ¼ cup of the sugar. Stir in chocolate and cook until melted. Remove from heat and add vanilla.

3. In a mixing bowl, beat egg yolks and remaining sugar until thick and pale yellow. Beat in coffee liqueur. Stir the warm chocolate mixture into the egg yolk mixture and blend well. In a mixing bowl, beat egg whites with salt until stiff. Gently fold the egg whites into the chocolate mixture. Pour batter into the pan. Bake 15 minutes.

4. For the sauce: Combine tequila and cajeta in a glass measuring cup; microwave 2 minutes, or until melted. Stir until smooth.

Finish

5. Unmold cakes onto a serving dish, and pour the sauce overtop.

Mocha Rum Brownie Bites

TYPE OF CAKE	SERVINGS	BAKING TIME	BOOZE METER	OCCASION
	24	40 to 45	☺	

Mocha Rum Brownies

1 (19.8-ounce) box brownie mix

2 eggs

2 teaspoons vanilla extract

¼ cup half and half

¼ cup brewed espresso or strong coffee

½ cup dark rum

½ cup (1 stick) unsalted butter, melted

Mocha Rum Frosting

Recipe on page 142

Finishing

24 fresh raspberries

Variations

Bourbon Brownie Bites with Chocolate Bourbon Frosting

For the frosting and cake: Substitute bourbon for rum and omit espresso.

Raw Chocolate Mocha Rum Brownie Bites

For the finishing: Instead of—or in addition to—the frosting, top brownie bites with wedges of high quality chocolate.

Brownie Bites with Candied Raspberries

For the finishing: Top frosted or raw chocolate-topped brownie bites with sparkling candied raspberries (page 136).

BOXED BROWNIE MIXES are plenty of people's dirty little dessert secret. Our brownie bites may start with packaged mix, but their flavor is boosted thanks to a couple not-so-secret ingredients: coffee and rum. Sometimes you just have to think outside the box!

Prepare

1. Preheat oven to 350°F. Grease a 9-by-13-inch baking pan.

Make

2. Combine all brownie ingredients and mix well. Pour into prepared pan and bake 40 to 45 minutes, or until a knife inserted in the center comes out clean. Let brownies cool completely before cutting into 24 equal pieces.

Finish

3. Top with generous dollops of frosting and raspberries. Arrange on a platter and let everyone dig in, family-style.

Mudslide Cake

TYPE OF CAKE	SERVINGS	BAKING TIME	BOOZE METER	OCCASION
🍰	(10) to (12)	⏰ 35	☺	👯 🎁 🥂

Irish Cream Cake
¼ cup strong espresso
¾ cup Irish cream liqueur
2¼ cups all-purpose flour
½ teaspoon baking soda
1 teaspoon baking powder
½ teaspoon salt
½ cup (1 stick) unsalted butter
¼ cup cocoa powder
1 cup sugar
1½ tablespoons vanilla extract
2 eggs

Irish Whipped Cream
2 cups heavy cream
¼ cup Irish cream liqueur

Irish Cream Caramel Sauce
¾ cup light brown sugar
5 tablespoons unsalted butter
⅓ cup heavy cream
1 teaspoon vanilla extract
¼ cup Irish cream liqueur

Garnish
¼ cup shaved chocolate or chocolate curls

FLAVORED WITH IRISH CREAM LIQUEUR, coffee, chocolate, and vanilla—the ingredients that constitute Baileys Irish Cream—this Irish cream cake is topped with rich Irish cream caramel sauce to make a delicious Mudslide of a cake. Top it with Irish-cream-infused whipped cream and a sprinkle of chocolate curls.

Prepare

1. Preheat oven to 350°F. Grease and flour two 9 inch cake pans.

Make

2. Combine espresso and Irish cream liqueur; set aside. In a bowl, combine flour, baking soda, baking powder, and salt. In a mixing bowl, beat butter, cocoa, sugar, and vanilla 3 to 5 minutes, or until light and creamy. Beat in eggs one at a time, and then mix 4 minutes, or until fluffy.
3. Add flour and Irish cream mixtures to the butter mixture in three alternating additions. Pour batter into pans and bake 20 to 25 minutes, or until knife inserted in the center comes out clean. Let cool completely.
4. For the whipped cream: Add cream and liqueur to a mixing bowl and beat until soft peaks form. Refrigerate until ready to use.
5. For the sauce: In a saucepan over medium heat, bring brown sugar, butter, and cream to a boil. Reduce to a simmer and stir about 5 minutes. Remove from heat and stir in vanilla and Irish cream liqueur.

Finish

6. Place one cake layer on a stand or serving platter. Spread half the whipped cream on top. Place the second layer on top, cover it with

The B-52 Cake

For the cake: Reduce the Irish cream liqueur to ¼ cup. Add ¼ cup coffee liqueur and ¼ cup triple sec. For the topping: Spike orange buttercream (page 119) with Grand Marnier instead of vodka and drizzle with spiked chocolate sauce (page 59).

Irish Coffee Cake

Replace the caramel sauce with homemade coffee liqueur (page 130) and dollops of whipped cream.

the rest of the whipped cream, sprinkle with shaved chocolate, and drizzle Irish cream caramel sauce all over.

7. For a crowd, scoop little Mudslide cake slices into individual party cups, pour Irish cream caramel sauce over top, and serve with big spoons.

THE LUCKY INVENTIONS OF THE IRISH

The Irish have a long history of inventing liqueurs. As early as the tenth century, they used alcohol as medicine, but within a couple centuries they were drinking it, imbibing whiskey for entertainment; by the fifteenth century, whiskey was ingrained in Irish culture. First brought to market by Baileys in 1975, Irish Cream was the first alcoholic drink to blend whiskey and double cream, boosted with hints of chocolate, vanilla, caramel, and sugar.

Try pairing smooth Irish Cream cocktails with your cakes:

B-52

1 ounce Kahlúa
1 ounce Irish cream liqueur
1 ounce Grand Marnier

In a glass layer Kahlúa, Irish cream, and Grand Marnier.

Mudslide

1 ounce vodka
1 ounce coffee liqueur (store-bought or homemade, page 130)
1 ounce Irish cream liqueur

Combine ingredients in a cocktail shaker filled with ice. Shake well. Strain into a glass over ice.

Wine-Tasting Cakes

TYPE OF CAKE	SERVINGS	BAKING TIME	BOOZE METER	OCCASION
🍸	㉔	⏰ 20 to ⏰ 25	☺	🍴◎🍷 🍸🍸 👥

Chocolate Merlot Cakes

1 cup (2 sticks) unsalted butter

2 cups sugar

4 eggs

1 cup merlot

2½ cups all-purpose flour

1½ teaspoons baking powder

½ teaspoon ground cinnamon

¼ teaspoon ground nutmeg

6 ounces dark chocolate, melted

Chocolate Merlot Icing

3 tablespoons unsalted butter

3 tablespoons unsweetened cocoa
   powder

¼ cup merlot

1¼ cups confectioners' sugar

1 teaspoon vanilla extract

Chardonnay Anise Cakes

¾ cup (1½ sticks) unsalted butter

1½ cups sugar

3 eggs, separated

1 teaspoon vanilla extract

½ teaspoon anise extract

2 cups all-purpose flour

1 tablespoon baking powder

¼ teaspoon salt

½ cup Chardonnay

½ cup milk

Chardonnay Anise Icing

3 tablespoons unsalted butter

1 cup Chardonnay

2 cups confectioners' sugar

½ teaspoon anise extract

HAVE YOU EVER PAIRED MERLOT with your favorite chocolate, or Chardonnay with your favorite spice? Food has been flavored with wine for centuries, but the concept of baking with wine is relatively new. These simple yet sophisticated cakes pair wines with complementary flavors. Substitute your favorite wines and spices and host your own special wine-tasting cake party!

Prepare

1.   Preheat oven to 350°F. Grease and flour two 12 cup cupcake pans.

Make

2.   For the chocolate merlot cakes: In a mixing bowl, cream butter and sugar 3 minutes, or until soft and fluffy. Mix in eggs and merlot. Add flour, baking powder, cinnamon, and nutmeg. Stir in chocolate. Pour batter into pans and bake 20 to 25 minutes. Let cool.

3.   For the chocolate merlot icing: In a saucepan over low heat, stir together butter and cocoa. Add merlot and confectioners' sugar, stirring until smooth. Remove from heat and stir in vanilla. Keep warm.

4.   For the chardonnay anise cakes: In a mixing bowl, beat butter and sugar 3 minutes, or until light and fluffy. Beat in egg yolks, anise, and vanilla.

5.   In a bowl, combine flour, baking powder, and salt. In another bowl, combine the wine and milk. Add flour and wine mixtures to the butter mixture in three alternating additions. In a clean mixing bowl, beat egg whites until stiff peaks form. Gently fold egg whites into the batter. Pour into pans and bake 20 to 25 minutes. Let cool completely.

6.   For the chardonnay anise icing: In a saucepan over low heat, warm butter until melted. Add chardonnay, confectioners' sugar, and

Finishing

White, milk, or dark chocolate curls

Star anise, anise seed, lavendar, fennel, or other herbs of your choice

Candied fruits or flowers (store-bought or homemade, pages 136 to 138), to complement a fruity wine

Cocktail picks or cupcake picks for easy nibbling

anise, stirring until the mixture has the consistency of a thin glaze. Keep warm.

Finish

6. Arrange cakes on a serving platter. Pour warm icings overtop, garnish as desired with fresh or dried herbs, white or dark chocolate curls, candied fruits or flowers, or cocktail picks, and serve immediately.

Variations

Blackberry Wine Cakes
For the cakes and icing: Omit chocolate. Soak ¾ cup blackberries in ⅓ cup blackberry wine for 1 hour. Drain the blackberries and add the wine to the cake batter. Add ½ cup blackberry wine to the icing.

Rosé Wine Cakes
For the cakes and icing: Replace chardonnay with rosé wine. Add ½ teaspoon rosewater to the cake and ¼ teaspoon to the icing.

Simple Merlot Cakes
For the cakes and icing: Omit chocolate.

4 Cakes with a Twist

POPULAR RECIPES SPIKED
with ALCOHOL

Want to make a good cake better? Bring in the booze! Here is a collection of popular cakes spiked with alcohol. Taste the gooey chocolatey goodness of Chocolate Lava Cakes oozing with Drambuie and Shamelessly Rich Carrot Cake spiked with 151-proof rum. Enjoy the campy fun of Lone Star Liquor Cake or cool down with a Spiked Ice-Cream Cake.

Black Jack Praline Cake

TYPE OF CAKE	SERVINGS	BAKING TIME	BOOZE METER	OCCASION
🍰	(8)	⏰50	☺	❄

Black Jack Cake
½ cup sugar
½ cup brown sugar
½ cup (1 stick) unsalted butter
3 eggs
1 tablespoon molasses
2¼ cups all-purpose flour
¾ teaspoon baking powder
1 cup canned sweet potato puree
¼ cup sour-mash whiskey
1 teaspoon cinnamon
½ teaspoon freshly grated nutmeg
1 cup pecans, toasted and chopped

Pecan Praline
¼ cup sugar
1 teaspoon molasses
1 tablespoon all-purpose flour
3 tablespoons unsalted butter
1½ cup pecans, toasted

Buttery Whiskey Sauce
¾ cup sugar
Pinch of salt
5 tablespoons unsalted butter
1 teaspoon vanilla extract
½ cup sour-mash whiskey

Variations
Brown Sugar Black Jack Cake
For the cake: Replace sugar, brown sugar, and molasses with 2 cups brown sugar.

WHEN THE NIGHTS GROW COOL and the leaves turn colors, it's time to pop this nutty whiskey-laced cake into the oven. It's a rich, spiced, sweet-potato creation topped with crumbly pecan praline and smooth buttery whiskey sauce.

Prepare

1. Preheat oven to 350°F. Grease and flour a 9-inch loaf pan. Toast pecans (2½ cups total for cake and praline topping) about 8 minutes in the oven as it warms, and then set aside.

Make

2. In a mixing bowl, beat sugars and butter 3 to 5 minutes, or until fluffy. Beat in eggs and molasses. Add flour and baking powder and mix until combined. Mix in sweet potato puree, whiskey, spices, and nuts. Pour batter into the pan and bake 50 minutes, or until golden brown.
3. For the praline: In a saucepan, combine sugar, molasses, flour, butter, and 1 tablespoon water. Cook over low heat, stirring until combined. Stir in toasted nuts.
4. For the sauce: In a saucepan over low heat, combine all ingredients and stir until the mixture reaches a gentle boil. Pour about one-fourth of the sauce over the cake.

Finish

5. Top cake with pecan praline and spoon the rest of the warm sauce overtop.

Brandy Apple Chai Cake

TYPE OF CAKE	SERVINGS	BAKING TIME	BOOZE METER	OCCASION
🍰	(10)	(60) *to* (65)	☺	☀ 🍴

Brandy Apple Cake
1½ cups canola oil
2 cups sugar
3 eggs
2½ cups all-purpose flour
⅛ teaspoon ground cloves
1¼ teaspoons ground cinnamon
½ teaspoon ground nutmeg
1 teaspoon baking soda
¾ teaspoon salt
1¼ cups walnuts, chopped
3¼ cups apples, peeled, cored,
   and chopped
¼ tablespoon brandy

Chai Glaze
4 tablespoons (½ stick) unsalted butter
2 tablespoons brown sugar
6 tablespoons sugar
3 tablespoons Voyant chai cream liqueur
2 tablespoons orange juice

Variations

Hard Cider Apple Cake
Replace brandy with hard cider. Replace chai glaze with buttery whiskey sauce (page 103).

Other Liqueur
If chai liqueur is unobtainable, substitute ½ teaspoon pumpkin pie spice added to 3 tablespoons Irish cream liqueur.

Pear Brandy Ginger Cake
Replace apples with pears. Add 1 teaspoon ginger. Use a pear brandy in the cake.

Whiskey Apple Cake
Replace brandy with whiskey. Substitute buttery whiskey sauce (page 103) for chai glaze.

CHAI IS AN AROMATIC SPICED DRINK that originated in India. This cake, chock-full of apples and walnuts, is topped off with a chai-spiced liqueur glaze. Cozy flavors of fresh apples, brandy, and buttery brown sugar are sure to warm you and your guests on a wintry night.

Prepare

1. Preheat oven to 325°F. Grease and flour a 10-inch Bundt cake pan.

Make

2. In a mixing bowl, beat oil and sugar until thick and smooth. Beat in eggs one at a time. Mix in flour, cloves, cinnamon, nutmeg, baking soda, and salt. Stir in walnuts, apples, and brandy. Pour into the pan. Bake 1 hour and 15 minutes, or until a knife inserted in the center comes out clean.
3. For the glaze: In a saucepan, melt butter; add sugars. Stir in chai cream liqueur and orange juice, and bring to a boil; reduce heat to low and cook 4 minutes.

Finish

4. Let cake cool 10 minutes, unmold, and pour warm chai glaze overtop.

Chocolate Lava Cakes

TYPE OF CAKE	SERVINGS	BAKING TIME	BOOZE METER	OCCASION
🍰🍩	⑥	⏰ 10 to ⏰ 12	☺	🎁 🥂 ♡

Chocolate Lava Cakes
1½ cups semisweet chocolate, chopped
5 tablespoons unsalted butter
3 eggs, separated
¼ cup sugar, divided
2 teaspoons port wine
1 tablespoon cocoa powder

Finishing
1 pint vanilla ice cream
3 tablespoons confectioners' sugar

CHOCOLATE AND A NIP OF PORT are surely one of life's little pleasures. These dark chocolate cakes are served fresh from the oven so that their port-flavored lava center is warm and gooey. Of course, you can use other spirits; just pair the chocolate with your personal favorite and enjoy!

Prepare

1. Preheat oven to 375°F. Grease and flour one large 6-cup muffin or cupcake pan or six (¾- to 1-cup capacity) ramekins or custard cups.

Make

2. Microwave chocolate and butter 2 minutes, or until the butter is melted. Stir and heat again until chocolate is melted completely and both are combined. Stir in egg yolks, 2 tablespoons of the sugar, and port. Set aside to cool slightly.
3. In a bowl, combine the remaining sugar and cocoa. In a mixing bowl, beat egg whites until foamy. Gradually add about 2 tablespoons of the sugar and cocoa, beating until soft peaks form. Gently fold the chocolate and sugar-cocoa mixtures into the egg whites in three alternating additions.
4. Pour batter into the pan and bake 10 to 12 minutes. The edges will be firm, but the centers will be a bit liquid. Cool 3 minutes before serving.

Finish

5. Run a knife around the edges. Invert onto serving plates and top with ice cream or a dusting of confectioners' sugar.

Chocolate Lava Cakes with Rum
For the cakes: Substitute dark rum for port.

Chococlate Lava Cakes with Spiked Whipped Cream
For the finishing: Instead of a side of ice cream, top cakes with spiked whipped cream (page 142).

Chocolate Lava Cakes with Whiskey
For the cakes: Substitute sour-mash whiskey for port.

Make-Ahead Chocolate Lava Cakes
For prepping the cakes: You can refrigerate the batter-filled pan, covered, up to 24 hours before baking. Extend the baking time by approximately 15 minutes.

Milk Chocolate Lava Cakes with Coffee Liqueur
For the cakes: Substitute milk chocolate for semisweet and coffee liqueur for port. (Learn how to make your own homemade coffee liqueur on page 130.)

A PORT PRIMER

Since the 1700s, the fortified wine that comes from northern Portugal has been called *vinho do porto*, or *porto* or simply *port*. Wines made in the same style are now made all over the world, including Argentina, Australia, South Africa, and the United States. Wherever it comes from, port is a wonderful thing not only to sip but also to bake with.

Port is made by adding brandy to wine and letting them age, boosting wine's sweetness as well as its alcohol content. The way the wine is aged impacts the taste and character of the port. Aging of wine is done either in sealed glass bottles, which is called "reductive aging," or in wooden barrels in a process referred to as "oxidative aging." Ruby port is a bottle-aged port. At two or three years old it is a younger port, fairly fruity, and typically less expensive. Tawny ports are aged in wood at least seven years, have a nutty flavor, and can cost a pretty penny. Vintage ports are rare, very old, and expensive. These are ports made from single superior vintages of grapes. White port is made from white grapes. There are several types, ranging from dry to sweet, within each port category.

Want to figure out what port you like best? How about a port-tasting party with friends? Each guest can bring a bottle for sampling. Break out the cigars and the chocolate lava cakes, and you'll have yourself a memorable evening.

Coffee Liqueur Cake

TYPE OF CAKE	SERVINGS	BAKING TIME	BOOZE METER	OCCASION
🍰	⑧	⏰ 55	☺	🌅 🍴☕🍸

Coffee Liqueur Cake

½ cup (1 stick) unsalted butter

1 cup sugar

2 teaspoons vanilla extract

2 eggs

⅓ cup coffee liqueur (store-bought or homemade, page 130)

1 tablespoon vodka

⅔ cup buttermilk

2 cups all-purpose flour

3 tablespoons unsweetened cocoa powder

2 teaspoons baking powder

½ teaspoon baking soda

¼ teaspoon salt

Coffee Liqueur Sauce

4 tablespoons (½ stick) unsalted butter

⅓ cup espresso or strong coffee

¼ cup coffee liqueur

2 cup confectioners' sugar

Finishing

2 teaspoons sweet ground chocolate, for dusting, if desired

½ cup chocolate-covered espresso beans, if desired

BREW YOUR FAVORITE ROAST for this coffee-infused cake. At small dinner parties, serve it family-style and encourage guests to help themselves from the cake platter in the center of the table.

Prepare

1. Preheat oven to 350°F. Grease a 9-by-3-inch loaf pan.

Make

2. In a mixing bowl, cream butter and sugar 3 to 5 minutes, or until light and fluffy. Beat in eggs and vanilla. In a another bowl, combine coffee liqueur, vodka, and buttermilk. In a third bowl, combine flour, cocoa powder, baking powder, baking soda, and salt.

3. Mix the flour and the buttermilk mixtures into the butter mixture in three alternating additions. Pour batter into the pan and bake 55 minutes, or until a knife inserted in the center comes out clean. Let cool.

4. For the sauce: Melt butter in a saucepan over medium-low heat. Stir in espresso and coffee liqueur. Add confectioners' sugar and stir until the mixture thickens into a sauce.

Finish

5. Pour coffee liqueur sauce onto a large platter. Place cake in the center. Dust with sweet ground chocolate or drizzle with additional coffee liqueur. Garnish with chocolate-covered espresso beans, if desired. Serve, spooning sauce from the platter over each slice.

Hazelnut Coffee Liqueur Cake
For the cake: Add 1½ cups chopped hazelnuts to the batter. Top with additional hazelnuts.

Toffee Coffee Liqueur Cake
For the cake: Add 1½ cups toffee pieces to the batter. Top with additional toffee pieces.

Mocha Chip Liqueur Cake
For the cake: Add 1½ cups chocolate chips to the batter. Top with chopped chocolate chips.

White Russian Coffee Liqueur Cake
For the cake: Omit cocoa powder, and increase vodka to 2 tablespoons; replace buttermilk with sour cream.

SUBSTITUTIONS FOR BUTTERMILK

Buttermilk, a slightly sour fermented milk, is an old-school ingredient. It's crazy, but back in the day, some people actually drank this thick sour stuff straight! Pure buttermilk is not appealing to most modern palates, but it is a dandy flavor addition to baked goods. And because few of us keep buttermilk in our refrigerators, here are some simple alternatives:

To make 1 cup buttermilk, substitute any one of the following:
- 1 cup milk + 1 tablespoon lemon juice
- 1 cup milk + 1 tablespoon white vinegar
- 1 cup milk + 1¾ tablespoons cream of tartar
- 1 cup water + 4 tablespoons powdered buttermilk

Stir ingredients together and let stand 10 minutes before using.

Alternatively, as a substitute for 1 cup buttermilk, use:
- 1 cup plain yogurt
- ¾ cup plain yogurt + ¼ cup milk
- ¾ cup sour cream
- ½ cup sour cream + ¼ cup milk

Deutsch German Chocolate Cake

TYPE OF CAKE	SERVINGS	BAKING TIME	BOOZE METER	OCCASION
🎂	⑩	⏰ 30 *to* ⏰ 35	☺	🎁 🍴 🥂

German Chocolate Cake
½ cup (1 stick) plus 4 teaspoons
   unsalted butter
1¼ cup sugar
3 eggs
3 teaspoons Jägermeister
1 teaspoon vanilla extract
½ cup unsweetened cocoa powder
1 teaspoon baking powder
½ teaspoon salt
1 teaspoon baking soda
2¼ cups cake flour

Coconut Pecan Frosting
1 (12-ounce) can evaporated milk
1½ cups sugar
¾ cup (1½ stick) unsalted butter
4 egg yolks
1½ teaspoons vanilla extract
4 tablespoons Jägermeister, plus a shot
   for the cook
2 cups shredded coconut, toasted
1½ cups pecans, chopped

Variation

**Double Chocolate Deutsch German
Chocolate Cake**

For the topping: For a sophisticated
edge, frost the sides of the cake with
chocolate frosting, or top it with curls
of dark chocolate.

CONTRARY TO WHAT YOU MIGHT THINK, German chocolate cake was not invented in Germany. A 1950s Texas housewife popularized a recipe using Baker's German's Sweet Chocolate, which was created by a guy named Samuel German in 1852. For fun, we've doctored the batter with every über-indulging rocker's favorite party shot: Jägermeister. *Prost!*

Prepare

1. Preheat oven to 350°F. Grease and flour two 8-inch round cake pans.

Make

2. In a mixing bowl, cream butter and sugar 3 to 5 minutes, or until light and fluffy. Beat in eggs. Add Jägermeister and vanilla.
3. Heat 1 cup water until warm. Combine cocoa, baking powder, salt, baking soda, and flour; mix it and the water into the butter mixture in three alternating additions. Pour batter into pans and bake 30 to 35 minutes, or until a knife inserted in the center comes out clean. Let cool.
4. For the frosting: In a saucepan over medium heat, combine evaporated milk, sugar, butter, egg yolks, vanilla, and Jägermeister. Stir 15 to 20 minutes, or until thick and golden brown. Remove from heat. Stir in coconut and pecans. Cool to room temperature for spreading consistency. Have yourself that shot of Jäger.

Finish

5. Frost one layer, stack the other layer on top, and frost again. No, this frosting won't stick to the sides, don't even try. And no, you better not have another shot of Jägermeister before the guests arrive.

Lone Star Liquor Cake

TYPE OF CAKE	SERVINGS	BAKING TIME	BOOZE METER	OCCASION
🍰	(14)	⏰20 *to* ⏰25	☺	🎁 🍸

Lone Star Liquor Cake
1 cup (2 sticks) unsalted butter
⅓ cup orange juice
4 tablespoons unsweetened cocoa powder
2 cups all-purpose flour
2 cups sugar
½ teaspoon baking soda
⅛ teaspoon baking powder
2 eggs
½ cup sour cream
1 teaspoon vanilla extract
⅓ cup Champagne
¼ cup bourbon
2 tablespoons cherry liqueur

Chocolate Champagne Glaze
½ cup (1 stick) unsalted butter
4 tablespoons unsweetened cocoa powder
½ cup Champagne
1 teaspoon vanilla extract
About 3 cups confectioners' sugar

Yellow Bourbon Buttercream
1 cup (2 sticks) unsalted butter
¼ teaspoon salt
2¼ cups confectioners' sugar
2 tablespoons bourbon
¼ cup half-and-half
A few drops yellow food coloring

Finishing
Lots of frosting, sprinkles, or boozy chocolate-covered cherries (page 138)

THIS SUPER-CHOCOLATEY RECIPE spikes the Lone Star State's signature cake—the Texas sheet cake—with the Texas Rose cocktail. It has the reputation for being so rich it can feed a Texas-size crowd. Channel your inner Texan and don't be shy about decorating with a generous scoop of sprinkles, boozy chocolate-covered cherries, or big, beautiful buttercream roses!

Prepare

1. Preheat oven to 375°F. Grease a jellyroll or sheet-cake pan.

Make

2. In a saucepan over medium heat, combine butter, orange juice, and cocoa, and bring to a boil. Let cool. Combine flour, sugar, baking soda, and baking powder in a bowl. Mix in cooled orange juice mixture, eggs, sour cream, vanilla, Champagne, bourbon, and cherry liqueur. Pour into the pan and bake 20 to 25 minutes.
3. For the glaze: In a saucepan over low heat, combine butter, cocoa, and Champagne and bring to a boil. Remove from heat and stir in vanilla. Add confectioners' sugar until glaze is thick but pourable.
4. For the buttercream: In a mixing bowl, beat butter until creamy. Add salt. Slowly add confectioners' sugar and bourbon. Mix in half-and-half as needed until fluffy. Tint with food coloring and refrigerate.

Finish

5. Pour glaze over the cake and let cool. Spoon the bourbon buttercream into a pastry bag or a plastic bag with one corner snipped off. Decorate the cake with loops, roses, or other fanciful toppings.

Rosemary Limoncello Cake

TYPE OF CAKE	SERVINGS	BAKING TIME	BOOZE METER	OCCASION
🎂	(8)	⏰(45)	☺	☀ ♡ 🛋

Limoncello Cake
¾ cup ground pine nuts, divided
½ cup (1 stick) unsalted butter
1 cup sugar
½ teaspoon vanilla extract
1½ teaspoons lemon juice
2 eggs
1¾ cups cake flour
2 teaspoons fresh rosemary, finely chopped
½ teaspoon baking powder
½ teaspoon salt
⅔ cup milk
2 teaspoons lemon peel, finely grated
3 tablespoons limoncello lemon liqueur

Limoncello Icing
1 cup confectioners' sugar
3 tablespoons limoncello lemon liqueur

Candied Lemon Slices
2 cups sugar
2 cups Meyer lemons, sliced thinly

Finishing
3 or 4 springs fresh rosemary

THE FLAVORS OF SUNNY SOUTHERN ITALY combine with a hint of fresh rosemary in this lovely lemony cake. It's baked in a thin *pignoli* (pine nut) crust, glazed with a light sweet-tart icing, and decorated with candied lemon slices. Limoncello is Sorrento's signature after-dinner digestivo, usually taken straight from the freezer and sipped in tiny glasses.

Prepare

1. Preheat oven to 350°F. Grease a 9 inch springform cake pan and dust with about ¼ cup ground pine nuts

Make

2. In a mixing bowl, beat butter 30 seconds; add sugar, vanilla, and lemon juice and mix 3 to 5 minutes, or until light and fluffy. Beat in eggs one at a time. Add flour, rosemary, remaining ½ cup pine nuts, baking powder, salt, and milk. Beat to combine.
3. Stir in lemon peel and limoncello. Pour batter into the cake pan and bake 45 minutes. Let cool.
4. For the icing: Stir sugar and limoncello together until consistency is spreadable.
5. For the lemon slices: In a saucepan, combine sugar with 2 cups water. Bring to a gentle boil and simmer 5 minutes. Add lemon slices and simmer another 5 minutes, making sure the fruit is soft but not falling apart. With a slotted spoon, remove lemon slices and cool on waxed paper.

Finish

6. Unmold cake onto a serving dish and pour glaze overtop. Decorate with candied lemon slices and a few sprigs of rosemary.

Screwdriver Cupcakes

TYPE OF CAKE	SERVINGS	BAKING TIME	BOOZE METER	OCCASION
🧁	⑫	㉑ to ㉓	☺	☀ 🪑

Scewdriver Cupcakes

3 eggs
¾ cup (1½ sticks) unsalted butter
1½ cups sugar
2 teaspoons orange zest
2½ cups all-purpose flour
2½ teaspoons baking powder
¼ teaspoon baking soda
⅛ teaspoon salt
½ cup orange juice
½ cup orange-flavored vodka
1 cup sweetened flaked coconut

Orange Vodka Buttercream

6 tablespoons (¾ stick) unsalted butter
2 cups confectioners' sugar
1½ teaspoons vanilla extract
3 tablespoons orange juice
½ cup heavy cream
3 tablespoons vodka

Finishing

½ cup sweetened flaked coconut,
    toasted or untoasted

Orange Curls

Zest of one orange

THESE SUNNY ORANGE CUPCAKES are made with toasted sweet coconut, fresh orange peel, and orange juice—plus a splash of orange vodka in the cupcakes and buttercream frosting.

Prepare

1. Preheat oven to 350°F. Grease and flour one 12-cup muffin or cupcake pan.

Make

2. Beat eggs until pale and foamy. In a mixing bowl, cream butter; mix in sugar and orange zest. Beat in the beaten eggs.
3. In a bowl, combine flour, baking powder, baking soda, and salt. In another bowl, whisk together orange juice and vodka. Add flour and vodka mixtures to the egg mixture in three alternating additions. Fold in coconut. Pour batter into the pan and bake 21 to 23 minutes. Let cake cool completely before frosting.
4. For the buttercream: In a mixing bowl, cream butter and sugar 3 to 5 minutes, or until light and fluffy. Mix in vanilla, orange juice, and cream. Fold in vodka.

Finish

5. Frost cupcakes with a generous amount of buttercream. Sprinkle with coconut, and then top with twisty orange curls.
6. For the orange curls: Use a peeler to cut strips of zest. Curl each strip by twisting it around a chopstick or drinking straw.

Shamelessly Rich Carrot Cake

TYPE OF CAKE	SERVINGS	BAKING TIME	BOOZE METER	OCCASION
🎂	10	45	☺	🎁 🥂

Shamelessly Rich Carrot Cake

4 eggs
¾ cup sugar
½ cup dark brown sugar
¾ cup vegetable oil
⅔ cup buttermilk
1 teaspoon vanilla extract
2 tablespoons amaretto
⅓ cup 151-proof rum
2 cups all-purpose flour
1½ teaspoons baking soda
½ teaspoon salt
½ teaspoon nutmeg
¼ teaspoon ground ginger
1 (16-ounce) bag carrots, peeled and shredded
1 (8-ounce) can shredded pineapple, drained
1 cup walnuts, chopped
½ cup raisins
1 cup sweetened flaked coconut

Maple Cream Cheese Frosting

½ cup (1 stick) unsalted butter
1 (8-ounce) package of cream cheese
3 cups confectioners' sugar
2 teaspoons orange zest
½ teaspoon vanilla extract
1 tablespoon maple syrup
3 teaspoons amaretto
2 tablespoons 151-proof rum

Finishing

8 to 10 marzipan carrots (page 140)

SPIKED WITH 151-PROOF RUM, this carrot cake lives up to its name—and then some. It's enriched with shredded carrots, pineapple, walnuts, raisins, and coconut and topped with a fluffy maple cream cheese frosting that's spiked with dark rum and amaretto.

Prepare

1. Preheat oven to 350°F. Grease and flour two 9-inch round cake pans.

Make

2. In a mixing bowl, cream eggs and sugars. Beat in oil, buttermilk, vanilla, amaretto, and rum.
3. In another bowl, sift together flour, baking soda, salt, nutmeg, and ginger. Gradually beat into the egg mixture with carrots, pineapple, walnuts, raisins, and coconut. Gradually add flour and carrot mixtures to the egg mixture in three alternating additions. Beat until just combined. Pour into the prepared pans and bake 45 minutes, or until a knife inserted in the center comes out clean. Let cool.
4. For the frosting: In a mixing bowl, beat butter and cream cheese until light and fluffy. Add confectioners' sugar, orange zest, vanilla, and maple syrup; beat until fluffy. Fold in amaretto and rum. Refrigerate frosting while cake cools.

Finish

5. Place one cake layer on a serving plate; slather it with frosting. Add the second layer and frost the entire cake. Garnish with marzipan carrots, if desired.

Spiked Ice-Cream Cake

TYPE OF CAKE	SERVINGS	BAKING TIME	BOOZE METER	OCCASION
🍩	⑩	⏰ 35	😃	🎈 🎁 🥂

Spiked Ice Cream
4 cups (2 pints) cherry vanilla ice cream, partially melted
¼ to ½ cup bourbon
A few drops food coloring, if desired

Bourbon Devil's Food Cake
½ cup (1 stick) unsalted butter
1¼ cups sugar
2 eggs
½ cup + 1 tablespoon unsweetened cocoa powder
1½ cups cake flour
¼ teaspoon baking powder
1 teaspoon baking soda
½ teaspoon salt
½ cup milk
¼ cup espresso or strong coffee
¼ cup bourbon

Creamy Vanilla Bourbon Frosting
1½ cups heavy cream
2 tablespoons sugar
½ teaspoon vanilla extract
2 tablespoons bourbon

HERE'S AN ADULT VERSION of everyone's favorite birthday cake. This recipe makes a chocolatey bourbon-laced cake that's filled with bourbon-spiked ice cream and topped with still more bourbon-infused frosting. You can experiment with any imaginable combination of cake, alcohol, ice cream, and frosting.

Prepare

1. Preheat oven to 350°F. Grease a 9- or 10-inch tube pan.
2. For the spiked ice cream: Stir together ice cream, bourbon, and food coloring; freeze overnight.

Make

3. Thaw spiked ice cream for 20 minutes or microwave on low in 60-second intervals until soft.
4. For the cake: In a mixing bowl, cream butter and sugar 3 to 5 minutes, or until light and fluffy. Beat in eggs.
5. Combine cocoa, flour, baking powder, baking soda, and salt; set aside. Combine milk, espresso, and bourbon. Beat the flour and bourbon mixtures into the butter mixture in three alternating additions. Pour the batter into the cake pan. Bake for 35 minutes, or until a knife inserted in the center comes out clean. Let cool completely.
6. For the frosting: In a mixing bowl, beat cream and sugar until light and fluffy. Stir in vanilla and bourbon.

Finish

7. Slice off the top fourth of the cake horizontally and set aside. Place the remaining cake on a freezer-safe plate. With a thin serrated

knife, gently score around the inner edge, about ¾ inch from the edge and no deeper than 1 inch from the bottom of the cake. Repeat with outer edge. With a serrated spoon, carefully scoop out the cake between the scores to create a tunnel. Freeze 1 hour. (Go for it! Eat the scooped-out cake while you're waiting.)

8. Remove the cake from the freezer. Fill the center tunnel with softened bourbon-spiked ice cream. Put the top layer back on, wrap tightly in plastic wrap, and freeze at least 4 hours. Frost, and then freeze 30 minutes before serving.

Variations

Flavor variations are endless! Try these combinations or mix and match to suit your taste.

Bourbon Chocolate Caramel-Vanilla Ice-Cream Cake

For the ice cream: Replace cherry vanilla with caramel vanilla swirl.

Champagne Pistachio Ice-Cream Cake

For the cake and ice cream: Bake Champagne cake (page 39) in a tube pan. Fill it with Champagne-spiked pistachio ice cream. For the frosting: Substitute Champagne for the bourbon.

Golden Rum Chocolate Ice-Cream Cake

For the cake and ice cream: Bake a golden rum cake (page 29) in a tube pan. Fill it with rum-spiked chocolate ice cream. For the frosting: Substitute rum for the bourbon and chocolate extract for the vanilla.

Rum Mocha Ice-Cream Cake

For the cake and ice cream: Prepare a chocolate cake in a tube pan. Add ½ cup rum to the batter before baking. Fill with coffee ice cream that has been spiked with rum. For the frosting: Substitute rum for the bourbon and chocolate extract for the vanilla.

Vodka Mint Chocolate Ice-Cream Cake

For the cake: Prepare a chocolate cake in a tube pan. Add ½ cup vodka to the batter before baking. Fill with mint chocolate chip ice cream that has been spiked with vodka. For the frosting: Substitute rum for the bourbon and mint extract for the vanilla.

FROSTY ICE-CREAM COCKTAILS

Scooped into a beverage or blended into creamy perfection, ice cream is a lovely addition to all sorts of cocktails. Here are a few to get you started:

Bourbon Fog

2 ounces bourbon

3 ounces coffee, hot or chilled
  (depending on the season)

1 scoop of ice cream

Combine bourbon and coffee; add ice cream. Supplement bourbon and coffee with amaretto, half-and-half, and chocolate syrup.

Death by Chocolate

1 cup crushed ice

1 ounce vodka

1 ounce crème de cacao

1 ounce coffee liqueur (store-bought
  or homemade, page 130)

1 ounce chocolate shavings

1 or 2 scoops chocolate ice cream

In a blender, mix all ingredients until smooth and creamy. Pour into a chilled glass, and top with whipped cream and a maraschino cherry if desired. *Swoon.*

Tres Leches Cake

TYPE OF CAKE	SERVINGS	BAKING TIME	BOOZE METER	OCCASION
🎂	(10)	⏰25	☺	🥂 🛖

Fluffy White Cake
½ cup (1 stick) unsalted butter
1 cup sugar
4 eggs, separated
1 teaspoon vanilla extract
1½ cups all-purpose flour
1 teaspoon baking powder
¼ teaspoon salt

Spiked Tres Leches
1 (14-ounce) can sweetened condensed milk
1 (7-ounce) can evaporated milk
1 cup milk
1 cup cachaça or rum

Spiked Whipped Cream
Use cachaça or rum in spiked whipped cream (page 142)

Variation
Fruity Tres Leches Cake
For the topping: Serve cake with maraschino cherries or fresh sliced strawberries. For a tropical flair, try mandarin orange wedges or pineapple chunks.

POPULAR IN LATIN AMERICA, Pastel de Tres Leches is a white cake soaked in three kinds of milk (*tres leches*) and topped with whipped cream. Once the dense cake has absorbed the milks, it becomes light, moist, and creamy. This version is soaked in cachaça, a Brazilian distilled spirit made from sugarcane that tastes more like vodka than rum, which also happens to be made from sugarcane. Cachaça (*kah-shah-sah*) is the alcohol in the famous Caipirinha (*kai-pi-rin-ya*) cocktail.

Prepare

1. Preheat oven to 350°F. Grease and flour a 9-by-13-inch cake pan.

Make

2. In a mixing bowl, cream butter and sugar 3 to 5 minutes, or until light and fluffy. Beat in egg yolks and vanilla. Mix in flour and baking powder. In a clean mixing bowl, beat egg whites until stiff and then fold into the batter. Bake 25 minutes, or until a knife inserted in the center comes out clean.

Finish

3. For the tres leches: Combine sweetened condensed milk, evaporated milk, and milk. Pierce the cake all over with a fork. Slowly pour milk mixture over the cake. Once the milk is completely absorbed, pour cachaça or rum overtop.
4. Top with spiked whipped cream and refrigerate at least 2 hours. Even when chilled, this cake is soft and moist. Cut individual squares from the baking pan and serve.

Homemade Booze

RECIPES FOR FLAVORED LIQUEURS AND HOMEMADE MIXERS

Some alcohol is easy to make from scratch. Take an alcohol base, add flavorings, seal it in a container, and then stash it for a while to steep and age. Come back in a month or so, and you've got a delicious homemade liqueur. Make sure your containers are clean, thoroughly dry, and sealed with airtight lids. Don't fill containers to the rim; give your booze some breathing room. From Coffee Liqueur to Sweet-and-Sour Mix, here are some simple recipes you're sure to enjoy.

Coffee Liqueur

1 (2-ounce) jar instant coffee
4 cups sugar
2 cups vodka or brandy
1 vanilla bean, sliced in half lengthwise

Boil 2 cups water, instant coffee, and sugar in a saucepan and stir until dissolved. Remove from heat and add vodka and vanilla bean. Transfer to an airtight jar and let sit in a dark place 30 days.

Makes about 2½ cups

Cranberry Liqueur

1 pound cranberries
2 cups sugar
4 cups vodka

Boil cranberries, 1 cup water, and 2 cups sugar in a saucepan 5 to 10 minutes, until berries start to pop. Remove from heat and let cool. Pour vodka into an airtight container. Add cranberry mixture and store in the refrigerator 1 week. Before using, strain out cranberries.

Makes about 5 cups

Crème de Menthe

3 cups vodka
2 cups simple syrup (page 133)
2½ teaspoons pure peppermint extract
1 teaspoon food-grade glycerine
1 tablespoon green food coloring, if desired

Combine all ingredients. Pour into an airtight container and refrigerate 2 weeks.

Makes about 5 cups

Eggnog

12 eggs, separated
1 cup sugar
8 ounces bourbon
8 ounces cognac
½ teaspoon salt
3 pints heavy cream
Freshly grated nutmeg, to taste

Beat egg yolks and sugar in a large bowl until light in color, about 3 minutes. Slowly mix in the bourbon and cognac while beating at low speed. Chill 3 hours.

Place the egg whites in a separate bowl, add salt, and beat to form peaks. Set aside. In a clean, chilled bowl, whip the cream until stiff, using clean beaters. Fold whipped cream and then beaten egg whites into the cream–yolk mixture. Chill 1 hour. Pour into a punch bowl, and sprinkle nutmeg on top. Serve in chilled mugs. For a thinner mixture, add 1 to 2 cups whole milk.

Makes about 30 servings

Flavored Vodka

2 cups vodka
½ cup fruit, cut in chunks, or fresh herbs, chopped

Put vodka and fruit or herbs in an airtight container. Refrigerate 2 weeks or longer, occasionally shaking the container. Before using, strain out fruit or herbs.

Makes about 2½ cups

Irish Cream Liqueur

1¾ cups Irish whiskey
1 (14-ounce) can sweetened condensed milk
1 cup heavy cream
2 tablespoons chocolate syrup
1 teaspoon vanilla
4 eggs
2 tablespoons espresso
½ teaspoon almond extract

Blend all ingredients in a food processor and pulse 15 to 20 seconds, or until smooth. Pour into an airtight container. Refrigerate up to 1 week.

Makes about 2 cups

Limoncello

10 lemons
3¾ cups vodka
5 cups simple syrup (page 133)

Wash lemons thoroughly and peel into long strips, being careful to avoid the white pith on the underside of the peel. Put lemon peel in a 2-quart airtight container and pour vodka overtop; steep unrefrigerated at least

MUDSLIDE CAKE
WITH IRISH CREAM CARAMEL SAUCE (PAGE 94)

1 week and up to 2 months (longer steeping time increases the flavor's intensity). Shake the container occasionally. After the steeping time, strain out the peels. Add simple syrup to the mixture; it will turn cloudy. Place in the freezer to let it age at least 1 week.

Makes about 4 cups

Simple Syrup

1 cup sugar

Bring 1 cup water and sugar to a boil in a small saucepan. Simmer, stirring until sugar dissolves, about 3 minutes. Remove from heat and allow to cool. Refrigerate in an airtight container. Simple syrup can be stored up to 1 month.

Makes about 1½ cup

Sour Cherries

¾ cup sugar
½ cup lemon juice
⅓ cup kirsch liqueur

Boil 1 cup water and sugar in a saucepan; stir to dissolve. Remove from heat and stir in the lemon juice and kirsch. Transfer to an airtight container and refrigerate up to 1 week.

Makes about 2 cups

Sweet-and-Sour Mix

1 cup sugar
1 cup lemon juice
1 cup lime juice

Boil 1 cup water; stir in sugar until dissolved. Remove from heat and add lemon and lime juices. Using a funnel, pour into an airtight bottle and refrigerate. Store chilled up to 1 month.

Makes about 3 cups

Homemade Treats

RECIPES FOR TOPPINGS, FROSTINGS, AND FANCY GARNISHES

Store-bought ingredients are quick and easy, but homemade goodies like Lavendar-Flavored Sugars, Cream Puffs, and Chocolate-Covered Cherries make desserts especially yummy. There's an added bonus: You can spike them with booze!

Candied Cherries

½ cup sugar
About 1 cup fresh cherries
Extra sugar for coating

Combine sugar and 1½ cup water in a saucepan and bring to a boil. Add cherries to the boiling sugar syrup and cook over medium-low heat, stirring occasionally, for 40 to 50 minutes or until soft but still intact. Place a wire rack over a baking pan to catch drips. Use a slotted spoon to transfer cherries to the rack to cool and dry overnight. Place extra sugar in a bowl. Dredge cherries in sugar to coat.

To store candied cherries, refrigerate in an airtight container between sheets of wax paper. If protected from heat, candied fruit can last as long as 6 months. Use ruby-like candied cherries to garnish drinks, cakes, cupcakes, and more.

Makes about 1 cup

Candied Flowers

Make sure the flowers are edible and organic. Some flowers are poisonous and should not be used. Common edible flowers that candy well include roses, violets, daisies, apple blosssoms, nasturtiums, and lilacs.

About 20 flower blossoms
2 egg whites
1 cup superfine sugar

Ensure the flowers are clean, dry, and free of blemishes. Place egg whites in a small bowl and whisk until frothy. Place sugar in a separate bowl. Using a pastry brush or small artist's brush, coat a flower with egg white, covering all the petals evenly. Dip the flower into the sugar and gently shake it to get rid of excess sugar. Place flower on a wire rack to dry. Finish the rest of the flowers the same way. You can store candied flowers in an airtight container for up to 1 month. Use them to garnish cakes, cupcakes, and elegant cocktails.

Makes 20 flowers

Candied Raspberries

½ cup sugar
About 1 cup fresh raspberries
Extra sugar for coating

Combine sugar and 1½ cup water in a saucepan and bring to a boil. Add raspberries to the boiling sugar syrup and cook over medium-low heat, stirring occasionally, for 40 to 50 minutes or until soft but still intact. Place a wire rack over a baking pan to catch drips. Use a slotted spoon to transfer raspberries to the rack to cool and dry overnight. Place extra sugar in a bowl. Dredge raspberries in sugar to coat.

To store candied raspberries, refrigerate in an airtight container between sheets of wax paper. If protected from heat, candied fruit can last as long as 6 months. Use candied raspberries to garnish drinks, cakes, cupcakes, and more.

Makes about 1 cup

Candied Rum Ginger

1 cup ginger, chopped
About 1 cup sugar
3 tablespoons dark rum

In a heavy saucepan over medium low heat, cover ginger with water, cook 30 minutes or until tender. Drain off water. Add sugar, rum, and 3 tablespoons water. Stirring constantly, cook over low heat until the ginger is transparent and almost all the liquid has evaporated. Let cool. Soak in additional rum, if desired. Then toss in additional sugar to coat. Let cool and firm up on a baking sheet 2 to 3 hours. Drizzle more rum overtop.

Makes about ½ cup

Candied Strawberries (Glacée Strawberries)

½ cup sugar
1 cup fresh strawberries, sliced
Extra sugar for coating

Combine sugar and 1½ cup water in a saucepan and bring to a boil. Add strawberries to the boiling sugar syrup and cook over medium-low heat, stirring occasionally, for 40 to 50 minutes or until soft but still intact. Place a wire rack over a baking pan to catch drips. Use a slotted spoon to transfer strawberries to the rack to cool and dry overnight. Place extra sugar in a bowl. Dredge strawberry slices in sugar to coat.

To store candied strawberries, refrigerate in an airtight container between sheets of wax paper. If protected from heat, candied fruit can last as long as 6 months. Use candied strawberries to garnish cakes, cupcakes, fruity cocktails, strawberry shortcakes, and more.

Makes about 1 cup

Chocolate-Covered Cherries

1 pound maraschino cherries
2½ cups confectioners' sugar, sifted
¼ cup (½ stick) unsalted butter
1 tablespoon corn syrup
1 teaspoon kirsch liqueur
2 pounds bittersweet chocolate

Drain cherries, reserving the syrup in a covered container. Refrigerate syrup until ready to use. Place cherries on a rack set over a baking sheet to dry overnight. To make the fondant: In a stand mixer, beat the butter until smooth and creamy. Add confectioners' sugar 1 cup at a time, and beat until it forms a smooth dough that is not sticky. Add corn syrup and 1½ tablespoons of the reserved cherry liquid, and mix until combined. Add kirsch and mix until combined.

Pinch off a small piece of fondant and roll it into a ball. Flatten it into a disc and place a cherry in the center. Wrap the fondant around the cherry to fully encase it. Repeat with the remaining cherries. Place on a baking sheet and refrigerate overnight until firm.

When you're ready to dip the cherries, melt the chocolate. Line a baking sheet with parchment paper. Dip the cherries in the chocolate and place on the sheet. Refrigerate dipped cherries for about 1 hour, or until the chocolate has set. Place cherries in an airtight container and store for 1 week before serving. Storage is the key to delicious chocolate-covered cherries; the centers need a week to liquefy. Use chocolate-covered cherries to top confections like the Black Forest Cupcakes (pages 23 to 24).

Makes about 60 cherries

Cream Puffs

⅔ cup unsalted butter
⅔ cup all-purpose flour
½ teaspoon salt
5 eggs, beaten
1 cup whipped cream or spiked whipped cream (page 142)

Preheat oven to 375°F. Grease baking sheets. In a saucepan over low heat, melt butter in 1⅓ cups water. Stir in flour and salt. Remove from heat and mix in eggs. Scoop tablespoonfuls of dough onto baking sheets and bake 15 to 20 minutes. When puffs are golden, turn off heat and open the oven slightly to cool them about 15 minutes. Transfer to a wire rack. Split cooled pastries with a knife and fill with whipped cream.

Makes 12 cream puffs

Chocolate Cream Puffs	Slice each cream puff in half and sandwich the halves with a spoonful of whipped cream. Drizzle with spiked chocolate sauce (page 59). Try not to eat all of these by yourself!

Flavored Sugars

2 cups confectioners', super-fine, or granulated sugar
1 vanilla bean, cleaned and dried

Vanilla	Put sugar in an airtight container, burying the vanilla bean inside. Seal the container and store it in a cool place at least 1 week. It will stay fresh for up to 3 months.
Lemon	Replace vanilla with zest of 3 lemons.
Orange	Replace vanilla with zest of 2 oranges.
Lavondar	Replace vanilla with ½ cup dried lavender buds.
Herbal	Replace vanilla with ¼ cup dried herbs, such as whole cloves, cinnamon sticks, or star anise.

Fluffy Marshmallow Crème

3 egg whites
2 cups light corn syrup
½ teaspoon salt
2 cups confectioners' sugar
1 tablespoon vanilla extract

Beat egg whites, corn syrup, and salt on high 10 minutes, or until thick. Add sugar and beat until well blended. Add vanilla and blend until combined. Store in airtight 2-quart container and refrigerate. Can be stored up to 1 week.

Makes about 2¼ cups

Gingersnaps

3 cups all-purpose flour
2½ teaspoons baking soda
¼ teaspoon salt
1 cup (2 sticks) unsalted butter
¾ cup sugar
¼ cup light brown sugar
½ teaspoon ground ginger

1 teaspoon ground cinnamon
¼ teaspoon white pepper
1 egg
⅓ cup molasses
Extra sugar for rolling

Preheat oven to 350°F. Line 2 baking sheets with parchment paper. Combine flour, baking soda, and salt in a bowl and set aside. Cream butter and both sugars until smooth. Add spices and mix until combined. Beat in egg and molasses. Add flour mixture and mix just to combine. Roll dough into 1-inch balls and roll in coarse sugar to coat. Place on baking sheets 2 inches apart. Bake 6 to 10 minutes, until light brown around the edges. Keep on baking sheet 5 minutes before transferring to a wire rack to cool. Store in an airtight container up to 4 days.

Makes 3½ dozen gingersnaps

Marzipan Carrots

½ cup store-bought marzipan
A few drops orange food coloring (or red and yellow)
A few sprigs parsley

Tint marzipan with food coloring and knead it until you have the desired shade. Pinch off small pieces, and roll them into cylindrical carrot shapes. Make an indentation in each carrot top with a toothpick and insert a sprig of parsley.

Makes about 1 dozen marzipan carrots

Meringues

3 egg whites, at room temperature
¼ teaspoon cream of tartar
1 cup sugar

Preheat oven to 250°F. Line a baking sheet with parchment paper. Using a mixer with the whisk attachment, beat egg whites on medium-low speed until foamy. Add cream of tartar and whisk on medium speed until soft peaks form. With the mixer running, add the sugar in a slow, steady stream and whisk until the meringue holds very stiff peaks. Dab a little meringue underneath the corners of the parchment paper on the baking sheet to act as a glue keeping the paper in place.

Fit a pastry bag with a ½-inch plain tip. Fill the pastry bag with half of the meringue. Pipe 2-inch mounds onto the sheet. Refill the bag, and pipe the rest. Bake 45 minutes to 1 hour. The meringues should not

SHAMELESSY RICH CARROT CAKE
WITH MARZIPAN CARROTS (PAGE 120)

color, but the outsides should become firm and dry. If they do not seem to be done after 1 hour, turn off the oven and leave them inside for another 20 to 30 minutes.

Makes about 1 dozen meringues

Mocha Rum Frosting

½ cup (1 stick) butter, melted
⅔ cup cocoa powder
3 cups confectioners' sugar
⅓ cup milk
1 teaspoon vanilla extract
1 to 2 teaspoons dark rum

Stir to combine butter and cocoa. Beat in confectioners' sugar and milk in three alternating additions. Add milk mixture to the butter and cocoa, along with vanilla and rum, stirring until smooth and creamy.

Makes about 3 cups

Spiked Buttercream

1 cup (2 sticks) unsalted butter
¼ teaspoon salt
3 cups confectioners' sugar
¼ cup bourbon, Champagne, or beverage of choice
¼ cup half-and-half

In a mixing bowl, beat butter and salt until creamy. Add confectioners' sugar and alcohol in alternating additions. Slowly add the half-and-half and continue beating until fluffy. Refrigerate until ready to use.

Makes about 3½ cups

Spiked Whipped Cream

3 cups (1 pint) heavy cream, cold
5 tablespoons sugar
2 tablespoons liquor, wine, or liqueur
Food coloring, if desired

In a mixing bowl, beat cream and sugar until stiff peaks form. Gently fold in liqueur with a rubber spatula. Tint with a few drops of food coloring.

Makes about 3 cups

Metric Conversions

Volume

U.S.	Metric
¼ tsp	1.25 ml
½ tsp	2.5 ml
1 tsp	5 ml
1 tbsp (3 tsp)	15 ml
1 fl oz (2 tbsp)	30 ml
¼ cup	60 ml
⅓ cup	80 ml
½ cup	120 ml
1 cup	240 ml
1 pint (2 cups)	480 ml
1 quart (2 pints)	960 ml
1 gallon (4 quarts)	3.84 liters

Length

Inches	Centimeters
¼	0.65
½	1.25
1	2.50
2	5.00
3	7.50
4	10.0
5	12.5
6	15.0
7	17.5
8	20.5
9	23.0
10	25.5
12	30.5
15	38.0

Weight

U.S.	Metric
1 oz	28 g
4 oz (¼ lb)	113 g
8 oz (½ lb)	227 g
12 oz (¾ lb)	340 g
16 oz (1 lb)	454 g
2.2 lb	1 kg

Oven Temperature

Degrees Fahrenheit	Degrees Centigrade	British Gas Marks
200	93	—
250	120	½
275	140	1
300	150	2
325	165	3
350	175	4
375	190	5
400	200	6
450	230	8
500	260	10

irreference \ir-'ef-(ə-)rən(t)s\ n (2009)

1 : irreverent reference
2 : real information that also entertains or amuses

HOW-TOS. QUIZZES. INSTRUCTIONS.
RECIPES. CRAFTS. JOKES.
TRIVIA. GAMES. TRICKS.
QUOTES. ADVICE. TIPS.

LEARN SOMETHING. OR NOT.

VISIT IRREFERENCE.COM
The New Quirk Books Web Site